Phoenix: The Full Story of Canada's Pay System Catastrophe

I0504452

Copyright © 2023 David Sabine.

All rights reserved.

ISBN: 9798393709457 — Paperback, 2023.
ISBN: 9781778006036 — Electronic book, 2023.

No portion of this book may be reproduced in any form without written consent from the publisher or author, except as permitted by Canadian copyright law.

This publication is designed to provide accurate and authoritative information regarding the subject matter covered. It is sold with the understanding that neither the author nor the publisher is engaged in rendering legal, investment, accounting, or other professional services.

While the publisher and author have used their best efforts in preparing this book, they make no representations or warranties with respect to the accuracy or completeness of the contents of this book and specifically disclaim any implied warranties of merchantability or fitness for a particular purpose. No warranty may be created or extended by sales representatives or written sale materials. The advice and strategies contained herein may not be suitable for your situation.

You should consult with a professional when appropriate. Neither the publisher nor the author shall be liable for any loss of profit or any other commercial damages, including but no limited to special, incidental, consequential, personal, or other damages.

Book cover art ("an exploding Phoenix and stacks of money in flame") by David × DALL·E (Human & AI).

Dedication

I dedicate this book to all Canadian taxpayers.

Acknowledgements

I am grateful to my wife, my daughters, my parents, and my siblings and their incredible children — it is an honour to be your husband, father, son, brother, and uncle.

I thank the journalists and my colleagues who reviewed pre-release versions of this book and offered their time and thoughtful feedback: Bill McClenny, Bogdan Steafan Plesa, Elizabeth Racz, Julie Ireton, Massimo Raimondi, Michael Bolton, Mike Caspar, Mike Edwards, Nima Honarmandan, Nina Tu, Wayne Hetherington.

I appreciate many others who engaged in conversation online regarding the vision, format, and cover design.

Thank you. Sincerely.

Contents

Disclaimer

I mix American style punctuation (e.g., quotes) with British style (e.g., commas).

"Hello," he said. ← American style punctuation.

'Hello', he said. ← British style punctuation.

"Hello", he said. ← Me.

I have included many footnotes, links, and references throughout the book. If you're a professor of a 100-level Bibliography course, take a deep breath — my formatting will anger you. I am consistent but I make up my own rules. For example: when I use others' material, I provide a footnote on the same page. I do this even if it means more than one footnote throughout the book citing the same source material.

Invitation

Please connect with me. Please like, share, and subscribe. Please publish reviews and critiques.

If you purchased a digital copy of this book, I offer a paper copy at a discount. And if you purchased a paper copy, I offer a digital version for free.

All at davidsabine.ca/phoenix

Foreword

The story of Canada's Phoenix Payroll debacle has been told by journalists, auditors, consultants, and federal employees.

One perspective is sorely lacking: an independent, digital systems management expert.

Like most Canadians, I watched the story unfold with astonishment, frustration, anger. I understand how *confusing* it can be and how difficult it must be to *believe* it.

How could this happen? People say.

I wrote this book because nothing about this tragedy *confuses* me and not only was it *believable*, it was *predictable*.

***

I anticipate my readers will be of these categories:

<u>Journalists</u>

For those of you willing to hold government to account, thank you for the work you do. I have written this book, in part, to help your reportage on this topic. I especially hope the chapters *Interlude*, *Possible Pasts*, and *Possible Futures*, provide valuable technical perspective.

<u>Parliamentarians</u>

For those of you willing to hold government to account, thank you for the work you do. You are in Parliament to represent taxpayers. I hope you find this book concise, clear, and helpful.

<u>Bureaucrats</u>

For those of you willing to hold government to account, thank you for the work you do. I hope this book helps you to avoid pitfalls and use taxpayers' funds more effectively in future.

Public Servants

If you have been adversely affected as Phoenix exploded, I hope this book provides perspective and answers to questions you may have, such as: Could it have been avoided? And will it happen again?

Tech Sector

Thank you for the work you do.

Let's uncover better ways.

Prologue

What would happen to you, to your family, if your employer stopped paying you?

They didn't terminate you. You can't collect Employment Insurance. They send paycheques, but for $0.00.

Imagine this carries on for a few months — then a few more. They tell you to call a specific phone number; you're told the people who answer that phone can fix things. But the phone is always busy and you've been waiting months for a callback.

Then, through news reports and conversations around the water cooler, you learn there are tens-of-thousands, just like you, calling the same number with similar problems. Similar, but not the same. You find out, while *your* paycheques amount to $0.00, *some* people have been *overpaid!*

First, you spend the maximum limit on all your credit cards. Then you cash in your savings to pay the balance on the cards. You've stopped buying fresh fruit and avoid driving more than required.

You max out the cards a 2nd time. Then sell the car to pay the balance. You visit the nearby foodbank to collect as much as possible, as often as possible.

Then you max out the cards a 3rd time and your mortgage hasn't been paid in months.

Your bankruptcy lawyer (the only person guaranteed to answer your call!) arranges to have your debts consolidated into an interest-only loan. A close relative agrees to pay the interest each month until you "get back on your feet".

Then a full year passes. Your employer is frequently in the news — you read a story about an employee who committed suicide and others whose marriages have collapsed.

Your house is being repossessed by the bank — your bankruptcy lawyer is doing everything possible to slow the process.

Now it's time to file your income tax forms.

Canada Revenue Agency (Canada's "tax man") instructs you to report the income you were *supposed* to get (not the amount you actually got). So, you do the math, file the forms, and they inform you tens-of-thousands of dollars are owing — taxes on the income your employer did not pay.

Not paying the tax bill will destroy what's left of your credit rating and invoke a legal battle you can't afford. But paying the tax bill will destroy what's left of your family's money: you will lose the house and the registered retirement savings.

***

Imagine that.

The extent to which each employee was and is affected by the Phoenix payroll tragedy varies. Through the personal accounts of those affected, we know:

- some sought new employment.
- some were overpaid and have had to repay overage amounts.
- some were underpaid and suffered severe financial hardship.
- some were underpaid but were sent demand letters claiming the opposite — they are having to "repay" money they never received.

- some were terminated due to displays of stress or anger in the workplace (i.e., "with cause" and therefore without access to Employment Insurance payments).
- some quit their job just to cash out pension funds to pay their debts[1].
- some have children who opted out of college because, as parents, they could not shoulder the cost of tuition or qualify for loans.

Throughout this book, I will chronicle the historical facts about the Phoenix payroll project; I will highlight key turning points where (I think) the catastrophe may have been averted; and I will share my insights as an experienced director and consultant of digital product organizations. As I do this, I hope the details, no matter how mundane, never distract us from the hardships and suffering of all those affected.

---

[1] Blacklocks Reporter. (2021, February 25). Phoenix Victim Loses House. Retrieved March 2, 2023, from https://www.blacklocks.ca/phoenix-victim-loses-house/, https://archive.is/HCsDD.

Present Day

It is winter as I write this. The year is 2023.

The Canadian Government has spent an estimated $4.2 billion (so far) on the implementation of a payroll system called "Phoenix".

With billions more to go and many years of litigation, the system has failed to successfully calculate paycheques for more than half of Canada's federal employees.

Some of those employees have lost their life savings, their home, their marriage, their dignity.

It's a catastrophe with no end in sight.

The Beginning

Sometime between 2009 and 2015, a few myopes in Canada's federal government gave the name "Phoenix" to one of their projects.

> **myope** noun
>
> my·ope: [ˈmī-ˌōp]
>
> : a nearsighted (myopic) person.

If you listen closely, you might hear the faint echoes: "One solution to rule them all", they said. "We'll save millions", they said. "We'll launch the new system with just the push of a button — the flick of a switch."

It isn't clear who coined the term, "Phoenix". And despite it being among the most ironic, regrettable monickers ever uttered for a government project, I'm quite sure they meant well.

We know only that the term was in use prior to 2015 by a department called Public Services and Procurement

Canada (PSPC)[2]. The term was supposed to be a motivating call to action for everyone involved in the new project, the goal of which was to *raise from the ashes* a new payroll apparatus. Phoenix would replace the aging payroll systems that the various federal departments had cobbled together over the years.

To understand why this new project was dubbed "Phoenix", a closer look at the events leading up to 2015 is required.

[2] Standing Senate Committee on National Finance. The Phoenix Pay Problem: Working Toward a Solution [PDF file]. Senate of Canada, 2018.
https://sencanada.ca/content/sen/committee/421/NFFN/reports/NFF N_Phoenix_Report_32_WEB_e.pdf, https://archive.is/sA7Wy.

The Very Beginning

Canada's federal government, like most large enterprises, began implementing digital systems as early as the 1960's. The earliest applications would perform complicated, redundant equations to reduce human error in areas of finance and administration such as payroll, accounting, and taxation.

While the applications were limited, procurement was not! By 1980, it is likely Canada's federal government had acquired several thousand computers. And for the purposes of this book, it is important to imagine the hodge podge of programs and computers in use across its various departments and agencies.

The period from 1960 (when US Department of Defence produced the COBOL language[3]) to 1980 (when Microsoft [Micro-Soft[4], at the time] started

---

[3] Micro Focus. (February 2022). What is COBOL? Retrieved March 2, 2023, from https://www.microfocus.com/en-us/what-is/cobol, https://archive.is/KA0Vz.

[4] Rubino, D. (2015, October 22). Where did the name Microsoft come from? Windows Central. Retrieved March 2, 2023, from https://www.windowscentral.com/where-did-name-microsoft-come, https://archive.is/Z4GPf.

development of MS-DOS[5]) was a period of rapid technological advancement.

In 1960, mainframe computers were expensive, huge, and rare. What we call "user interaction" today was impossible. There was no "interacting" with the computer interface — people created programs on paper punch cards and controlled their computers with giant push-button consoles.

Data storage was time-consuming and was achieved by recording sequences onto magnetic tape with large reel-to-reel tape machines. It was as expensive as it was unreliable — get those tapes too close to a magnet or heat source and all data would be lost.

But in the years that followed:

- Transistors shrunk in size and grew in capacity.
- The mouse was invented in 1964. In the same year, the BASIC language became generally available.
- University students could study COBOL, FORTRAN, and BASIC while listening to The Doors or The Beatles' Magical Mystery Tour.

---

[5] Digital Research. (n.d.). HISZ - High speed data compression. Retrieved March 2, 2023, from http://www.digitalresearch.biz/HISZMSD.HTM, https://web.archive.org/web/20171002211831/http://www.digitalresearch.biz/HISZMSD.HTM.

- The APRAnet's (an early name of the internet) first hosts were connected in 1969[6].
- Hewlett-Packard figured out how to make a calculator small enough to be carried — math students rejoiced!
- The video game craze began in 1979 with the release of Space Invaders.
- And in 1980, the world's most popular personal computer was the TI-99 from Texas Instruments.[7]

With every advancement and the release of each new computer, whole ecosystems of new software applications and programming languages would follow.

Bureaucrats and high-priced consultants worked tirelessly to implement every new-fangled device and fancy program. Each year during budget season, grand plans were forged to "modernize" the office and purchase all the latest gadgets.

[6] Ghose, T. (2012, April 23). Who invented the Internet? Retrieved March 2, 2023, from https://www.livescience.com/20727-internet-history.html, https://archive.is/k5sQe.
[7] Statistics Canada. (2019, June 10). The history of statistics in Canada. Retrieved March 2, 2023, from https://www150.statcan.gc.ca/n1/edu/power-pouvoir/ch4/history-histoire/5214792-eng.htm, https://archive.is/W6Bv2.

If you, my dear reader, have experience writing software with at least a few languages and/or have inherited the software written by others, then I am confident you can understand the house of cards the Canadian government puzzled together in those 20 years.

But if you do not have such experience or you've ever thought it difficult to maintain the optimal collection of charging cables as new smartphones are released, then I'm afraid you may not be equipped to behold the cacophony that was the daily experience of back-office administrators and IT staff through the 1980's.

First, imagine a snafu. Then light a dumpster fire. Throw in a fubar. The word clusterf* isn't strong enough. Massacre and omnishambles are too polite. Top it off with a hot mess, a pinch of disaster, and a dash of trainwreck.

The Mulroney Era

Brian Mulroney, Canada's 18th Prime Minister, took office in 1984.

*****

David Lee Roth was Van Halen's lead singer. Michael Jackson's *Thriller* was the best-selling album. Cyndi Lauper told us *Girls Just Want to Have Fun.* Prince released *Purple Rain.* The Tragically Hip, then called the Rodents, played their first gigs in eastern Ontario.

*****

Mulroney's time in office is remembered with mixed reviews. Despite being leader of a conservative party, he introduced one of Canada's most burdensome taxes: the GST. He enabled the privatization of two federal crown corporations: Air Canada and Petro-Canada. His record on human rights was strong; he was outspoken against apartheid in South Africa and developed a noteworthy relationship with Nelson Mandela. He was first elected with record-breaking support but left the office with the lowest approval rating of any previous Prime Minister. *Et cetera*.

We must imagine that, while he held office, bureaucrats in all federal departments would complain, *daily*, about the technical challenges they faced.

He would have learned how expensive it had become to manage large mainframes. He would have heard buzzwords like "n-tier systems" and "client-server architecture" and "Moore's Law". His technical staff would have argued the pros and cons of "SLED" storage versus "RAID" arrays. He would have fielded questions from reporters about his plans to automate manual processes and modernize government offices. He would have been briefed about the potential uses of new "protocols" called "TCP/IP" and "DNS" and "the Internet". His advisors would have used words like "cyberspace" and "information highway" to illustrate the impending technological revolution.

Despite the growing technological chaos in government offices, it is not surprising he largely ignored the problem through his first term in office. A newly elected Prime Minister is bound to act on big-ticket campaign promises. For Mulroney, those promises included carving a special place in Canada's constitution for Quebec, a free trade deal with the United States, and tackling high inflation and debt inherited from his predecessor, Pierre Trudeau.

From my perspective, with hindsight, ignoring the IT (Information Technology) problem was the right thing to do — because solutions were not obvious. Ideas were plentiful but none would have been future proof; the horizon of predictability had shrunk from many years to just a few months.

For example: if you were tasked, in 1984, with procuring telephones for government offices, all the available options had standard earpieces, standard dial-pads, and would continue to function even in the present day (plugged directly into copper wirelines or Voice-over-IP adapters). The horizon of predictability in this case can be measured in decades.

But the horizon of predictability with respect to programming languages, data storage format, network device speed and compatibility, there were no standards...only bets. Everything was a gamble. Technology was changing so rapidly that any solution conceived in 1984 would be obsolete by 1985, and (likely) unmaintainable soon thereafter.

***

Then, in 1988, voters granted Mulroney's government a 2nd term.

Sammy Hagar was Van Halen's new lead singer. Belinda Carlisle told us *Heaven Is a Place on Earth*. The Tragically Hip was preparing to record their seminal album, *Up To Here*. And Rick Astley's *Never Gonna Give You Up* became Billboard's #1 hit on March 12[8].

Having already addressed the lowest-hanging fruit and having the luxury of four more years, Mulroney's cabinet must have felt an urge to address deeper challenges. Perhaps they had grown confident to tackle more contentious, systemic dysfunctions such as the IT operation.

The payroll and pension systems caught their attention. In 1989 (June, by some accounts), Mulroney's government announced they would study ways to replace legacy pay systems.

---

[8] Billboard. (n.d.). Rick Astley. Retrieved March 2, 2023, from https://www.billboard.com/artist/rick-astley/.

I will spare you, my dear reader, the boring details. Suffice to say committees were struck, reports were prepared, recommendations were offered, consultants were hired, requirements were gathered, estimates were provided, and proposals were made.

For almost four years, the machinery of government bureaucracy plodded along — it offered promises and solutions. "At the click of a button", they would say. "Cheaper, better, faster!"

Then, would you be surprised to learn a $45 million contract was awarded mere weeks before the 1993 election was called?

But hold on. Before you and I wonder if that timing is curious, let us consider the context:

- Brian Mulroney's popularity had plummeted, reaching only 12% at its lowest point[9].
- He stepped down[10] in June 1993 and Kim Campbell became Prime Minister. (As an aside, while this may cause some readers much

[9] The Canadian Encyclopedia. (n.d.). Brian Mulroney. Retrieved March 2, 2023, from https://www.thecanadianencyclopedia.ca/en/article/brian-mulroney, https://archive.is/Ue1v4.

[10] Fletcher, T. (1993, February 25). Mulroney declares intention to resign. The Washington Post. Retrieved March 2, 2023, from https://www.washingtonpost.com/archive/politics/1993/02/25/mulroney-declares-intention-to-resign/94ede77d-83d7-4f69-bc54-fea49b346d28/, https://archive.is/QhRMy.

cognitive dissonance, Canada's first female Prime Minister was a conservative.)

- Kim Campbell's approval rating was very high – the highest level for a Prime Minister in 30 years – but it did not look likely her party would win the forthcoming election.

We can therefore conclude the bureaucrats managing the payroll and pension modernization project – the crew that had already spent four years on the portfolio – were eager to get signatures on a contract before their budget would evaporate.

And so it went, in August 1993, a contract was signed with Accenture to automate the work performed by ~750 payroll staff[11].

But, please read on to learn how that contract would become the ashes from which the so-called Phoenix would rise.

---

[11] Bagnall, J. (2018, February 24). Risks unheeded, journey without end: The seeds of the tortured Phoenix pay project were planted three decades ago. Ottawa Citizen. Retrieved March 2, 2023, from https://ottawacitizen.com/news/politics/risks-unheeded-journey-without-end-the-seeds-of-the-tortured-phoenix-pay-project-were-planted-three-decades-ago, https://archive.is/vK758.

The Chrétien Era

Jean Chrétien, Canada's 20th Prime Minister, took office in 1993.

***

Sammy Hagar was still Van Halen's lead singer. Nirvana released what would be their final album, *In Utero*. Whitney Houston's *I Will Always Love You* brought tears to our eyes. And Canadians across the country saw The Tragically Hip at the travelling summer festival, *Another Roadside Attraction*.

***

Like his predecessor, Chrétien's time in office is remembered with mixed reviews. He began with decisive victory and ended with scandal.

Chrétien's contribution to the Phoenix payroll debacle was crucial:

1. In 1993, his government introduced the "Long Gun Registry". (This decision, as we will see, becomes critically important to our story twenty years later.)
2. And in April 1995, Jean Chrétien's government burned the contract with Accenture.

Nothing left but ashes! (And a giant lawsuit.)

***

Why did the government terminate Accenture's contract? James Bagnall, with the *Ottawa Citizen*, offered an explanation in February 2018. His explanation starts like this:

> "First, the Accenture effort was a custom-built system...Accenture was also modernizing two systems in one go – pay and pensions.
>
> Second, the government had awarded a fixed-price contract, which meant that when glitches emerged in development, Accenture was forced into difficult trade-offs: To stay within budget, it had to either

eliminate certain software features or try to make the case for a revised contract."[12]

Bagnall goes on to explain Accenture had done just that: they tried to renegotiate their contract to include more money and time.

I see the situation in simpler terms: the contract with Accenture was a fool's errand and burning it was a good decision.

Doomed from the outset, ending the contract probably saved Canadian taxpayers huge sums of money. My only advice to Canada's government, if I were involved, would have been to end the contract sooner.

(I will explain my position further in an upcoming chapter called *Possible Pasts*.)

Please, my dear reader, understand it gives me no pleasure to complement the scandal-plagued Chrétien cabinet. But I give credit where it's due: they did the right thing in this case.

---

[12] Bagnall, J. (2018, February 24). Risks unheeded, journey without end: The seeds of the tortured Phoenix pay project were planted three decades ago. Ottawa Citizen. Retrieved March 2, 2023, from https://ottawacitizen.com/news/politics/risks-unheeded-journey-without-end-the-seeds-of-the-tortured-phoenix-pay-project-were-planted-three-decades-ago, https://archive.is/vK758.

Unfortunately, predictably, Accenture's lawyers took the government to court within a year of the contract's termination — the legal battle was finally settled in 2003, Jean Chrétien's last year in office.

The details of the settlement are not known to the Canadian public. It is rumoured Accenture was paid between $20 – $45 million.

The Martin Era

Paul Martin, Canada's 21st Prime Minister, took office in December 2003.

***

The Tragically Hip was touring with an album called *In Violet Light*. Beyoncé was *Crazy in Love*. 50 Cent was making millions. And Van Halen's lead singer was Gary Cherone (this did not catch on).

***

Paul Martin's time in office is remembered with mixed reviews. (I detect a pattern.) After taking office in 2003, he called a federal election in 2004 hoping his Liberal party would form another *majority* government for a 4th term. They did not.

The Liberals formed a *minority* government on shaky ground[13]. Most people appreciated that Martin balanced the budget but he could not escape the lingering effects of "the sponsorship scandal" (as it was called).

With respect to our story about the payroll and pension systems, there is nothing more to say about Paul Martin. The legal battle with Accenture was done and nobody wanted to approach that topic for a while.

Martin spent the next two years trying to wrangle a minority government then lost the next election.

---

[13] Encyclopædia Britannica. (n.d.). Paul Martin. In Encyclopædia Britannica. Retrieved March 2, 2023, from https://www.britannica.com/biography/Paul-Martin, https://archive.is/vs3ua.

The Harper Era, 1st Term

Stephen Harper, Canada's 22nd Prime Minister, took office in January 2006.

***

The Tragically Hip released a new album, *World Container*, and the single, *In View,* hit #1 on Canadian charts. Gnarls Barkley went *Crazy.* Maybe you remember Nickelback's *Photograph*? And would you believe there were rumours circling that David Lee Roth might return to Van Halen? (I am not making this up!)

***

Harper's time in office is remembered with (you guessed it) *mixed reviews.* Most people agree his government handled the 2008 financial crisis better than most. He promised to cut the GST by 2% and he did. But his party stuck their own feet too many times into their own mouths and he was eventually ousted from the Prime Minister's office in 2015.

I know we are already many pages and a few chapters into this little book — but it is just now that we can turn our attention to the Phoenix.

I first wanted to tell you of the four Prime Ministers, the two decades, the countless scandals, and the $45 million contract that went up in smoke. I trust we both can understand how the politicians, bureaucrats, project managers, and IT personnel could refer to their payroll and pensions systems as "a bed of ashes".

When Stephen Harper took office, payroll staff across the country told parliamentarians of incredible technological clutter and dysfunction. IT administrators were up to their ears in bug reports and service calls. Many employees were younger than their payroll systems. (Fax machines, dot-matrix printers...in 2006!)

It was in this context the Phoenix project was conceived. The mental image of a Phoenix was compelling. It was aspirational, motivating. But would it take flight?

2007, February

With a new Prime Minister in office, and Accenture's lawsuit long forgotten (by most), there seemed a renewed appetite to improve the federal payroll systems.

IBM produced a report for Government of Canada called *Pay Benchmarking Study*. It is not publicly available (to my knowledge) but is referenced by Julie Ireton of CBC in an article ten years later. She noted that IBM strongly recommended "off-the-shelf" software — IBM claimed they are "consistently more cost effective and enable higher quality and efficiency, when implemented and sustained properly".[14] In other words, IBM advised Canada's government *against* producing tools in-house. In three words, they were saying: *Buy. Don't Build.*

***

[14] Ireton, J., CBC News, "Phoenix pay fiasco: Conflict of interest concerns raised over IBM, PwC's early work," CBC, September 26, 2017, https://www.cbc.ca/news/canada/ottawa/phoenix-conflict-of-interest-ibm-pwc-early-work-pay-fiasco-1.4327089, https://archive.is/gpOC2.

An aside...

IBM's report was persuasive or their advice mirrored the prevalent mindset of bureaucrats at the time. Either way, you will see in upcoming pages that Canada's government leaned into this recommendation. The notion that all pay systems must be replaced by a COTS product (Commercial Off The Shelf) was all-consuming. All other options were categorically rejected.

But I confess: I may have made the same recommendation at the time. In 2007, many new products were on offer, tech companies were booming, and it was easy to have inflated confidence in their quality and customizability.

But IBM's consultants, at the rates they charge, should have been smarter than *younger me*. Their recommendation, in my opinion, is problematic for three reasons:

- Of the companies that had relevant COTS products in the market, most were high-risk fast-growing startups and only a few were backed by companies with proven longevity.

- The software market was extremely volatile and in the throes of massive disruption from rapid growth in OSS (open-source software). How did IBM factor this into their recommendation? *(Let's just say I have questions.)*
- The very concept of a COTS was still a novelty and long-term studies were extremely rare and niche. (In other words, I don't know how IBM reached the conclusion that COTS are "consistently more cost effective and enable higher quality and efficiency". I doubt they were challenged to produced more than a few cherry-picked case studies.)

2007, June

Members of Parliament were hearing of a backlog of 2,000 employees who received paycheques with incorrect amounts. They were hearing that new federal employees would wait three months before getting their first paycheque. They were hearing of high turnover in payroll staff.

Alarm bells were ringing.

In 2007, the Standing Committee on Government Operations and Estimates (OGGO) undertook "a study" (this is an official type of committee activity) of the "Employee Compensation Delivery System" and heard from witnesses including delegates from the treasury and payroll staff[15].

The committee believed that payroll operations were outdated and prone to error — they questioned the witnesses to that effect. I shall spare you the tedious work of reading committee evidence and meeting minutes.

In summary...

In a meeting on June 5, 2007 (were you to examine the same boring documents that I have), you would find that Canada's federal government employed roughly 186,000 people.

You would find neither the witnesses from the Treasury nor Public Service Agency could provide detailed information about the alleged deficiencies. They repeatedly denied there was a widespread problem.

---

[15] Canada. Parliament. House of Commons. Standing Committee on Government Operations and Estimates. (n.d.) Meeting Nos. 55, 56. 39th Parliament, 3rd Session. Retrieved March 2, 2023, from https://www.ourcommons.ca/Committees/en/OGGO/StudyActivity?studyActivityId=2118698, https://archive.is/6d87u.

Instead, they spoke of "pockets" where problems had occurred.

You would find that approximately $108 million annually was spent to employ roughly "2,100 employees in the compensation community" and their average salary was $51,700. This, according to Rick Burton, a Vice President in Human Resource Management[16].

"Compensation community"!?

Yes, that is how some bureaucrats talk.

With a rare bit of humour, Member of Parliament Raymond Simard, asked "Why don't we call them staff?"

¯_(ツ)_/¯

Three patterns are apparent in the committee's transcripts:

- The witnesses downplayed the errors.
- They advocated for more staff. Hélène Laurendeau, of the Treasury, explained they

---

[16] Canada. Parliament. House of Commons. Standing Committee on Government Operations and Estimates. (n.d.). Evidence. 39th Parliament, 1st Session. Meeting 55. Retrieved March 2, 2023, from https://www.ourcommons.ca/DocumentViewer/en/39-1/OGGO/meeting-55/evidence, https://archive.is/B51FL.

wished to make "extra effort to make sure that we recruit and train and equip the people so that we do not fall behind".

· The dialogue circled around the idea that centralization of the payroll function would be a good thing. Without evidence to support that notion, they all had the same movie playing in their minds about *one system to rule them all.*

Rick Burton:

"...we're looking heavily to the use of technology...we've done a lot of work to help the compensation advisors themselves do their work with an application called *virtual pay*...but we haven't looked at a system-wide HR system that will capture all this from all departments. Many departments have their own homegrown systems. And we have a very powerful initiative under way now to try to consolidate them in one information system."

Daryl Kramp:

"It would make sense."

Rick Burton:

"It makes perfect sense."

***

My dear reader, please look forward to an upcoming chapter I call *Possible Pasts* where we will ponder these questions: Did they forget that their existing systems were *successfully* paying 184,000 employees? (That is a 99% success rate.) Were the committee members curious to learn which "pockets" were getting it *right*? Or did they rush to a conclusion that all systems must be replaced with one centralized behemoth?

***

Days later in a meeting June 7, 2007, you would find:

John Gordon, President of the federal employees' union, declared the payroll and pensions systems needed "a complete overhaul". He also supported a suggestion that the function of pension administration be centralized in Shediac, New Brunswick. And he argued the payroll staff should be paid more[17]. (Such is a union president's default position.)

I am loathe to agree too easily with a union boss, but other witnesses elaborated on this issue of salary, providing helpful nuance.

Diane Melançon, a compensation advisor (*someone who actually does the work!*), explained that her colleagues enjoyed their work most (and stayed in the job) when they felt good about their work: "...most of us, the compensation advisors, the people I know, are very hard-working people. We care about giving excellent service. We don't believe in your calling this telephone line and getting a ticket number."

She also described a growing frustration among her colleagues. Compensation advisors enjoyed their work when they felt a relationship with the people they helped day-to-day, but a change in management was upon them. Their work was being forcibly compartmentalized — lines, that to the employees felt arbitrary, were being drawn through their duties.

---

[17] Languages. (n.d.). Evidence. 39th Parliament, 1st Session. Meeting 56. Retrieved March 2, 2023, from https://www.ourcommons.ca/DocumentViewer/en/39-1/OGGO/meeting-56/evidence, https://archive.is/JIxpP.

Melançon explained:

> "they are told, from now on all you're going to be
> doing is *promotions*, that's it, that's all. They leave
> those departments. They go to departments where
> they can do *all* the duties they're normally expected
> to do...they don't want to lose expertise."

Susan Louis-Seize, another compensation advisor,
expanded on this concern:

> "...can the tasks be divided? The problem with
> dividing the tasks into *pay* or just *pension* or just
> *insurance* is that they are all interrelated, and it
> would create an area for error."

***

As an aside: In a meeting months later, the committee
would hear further evidence of this from Jill Ronan,
another compensation advisor:

> "Some departments attempted to go to things like
> *single discipline*...where they broke up the team and
> went to full-blown call centres. It's interesting to

note that they were the ones that ended up with the biggest backlogs."[18]

Let us return to June 7...

***

The witnesses further explained it would take two years to hire and train new compensation advisors. And 60% of those would leave within the first two years. Michael Brandimore, a compensation advisor, shared with the committee: "the workload is so staggering...they realize what's in store, and they're saying thanks, but no thanks."

Louis-Seize relayed perhaps the most important information of the day (paraphrased):

> "I'd like to give a little bit of history...Since 1997 we have had a lot more policy changes, a lot more collective agreement changes...a growing number of policies.

---

[18] Canada. Parliament. House of Commons. Standing Committee on Government Operations and Estimates. "Evidence." 3 Mar. 2021, 39th Parliament, 2nd Session, Meeting 10. https://www.ourcommons.ca/DocumentViewer/en/39-2/OGGO/meeting-10/evidence, https://archive.is/DmcWQ.

...we have over 72 collective agreements. We have over 70,000 rules and regulations...

If we look back at the pay records of 1970, it was a walk in the park. They came, they arrived, there were no rules and regulations. But as government changed and policies came into play, it got more and more complex over time with all the collective agreements."

***

My dear reader, I will intentionally withhold advice until future chapters. Our goal in these early pages is to understand the events as they unfolded. But, in *this* moment, let's make a mental note about the testimony of these employees.

Did they describe their colleagues as hard-working people who "care about giving excellent service"? Did they attribute errors/problems in their work to dysfunctional software — or did they describe a work environment in which complexity was growing while the humanness of the work was diminishing?

2007, December

December 10, in a meeting of the same OGGO committee, the Chairperson broke from the agenda[19] to question a witness about payroll errors. Nearing the end of the meeting, Diane Mireau said, "...this is a pet project of mine. It's about employee compensation. The last time you appeared before the committee you had a tremendous backlog of issues on compensation. I'd like to know what's happening within the public works department on compensation at this time. How big is the backlog?"[20]

MP Michael Fortier was the first to respond.

> "The backlog is actually much, much smaller than it was...We had people working overtime. We had outsourced part of the job...we've really dealt with a very large segment of the backlog and I'm hopeful that in the very near future this won't be a problem."

---

[19] Canada. Parliament. House of Commons. Standing Committee on Government Operations and Estimates. (n.d.). Notice of meeting. 39th Parliament, 2nd Session. Meeting 7. Retrieved March 2, 2023, from https://www.ourcommons.ca/DocumentViewer/en/39-2/OGGO/meeting-7/notice, https://archive.is/Pbgv2.

[20] Canada. Parliament. House of Commons. Standing Committee on Government Operations and Estimates. "Evidence." (n.d.). 39th Parliament, 2nd Session, Meeting 7. https://www.ourcommons.ca/DocumentViewer/en/39-2/OGGO/meeting-7/evidence, https://archive.is/QBBsw.

To corroborate, François Guimont, Deputy Minister of Public Works and Government Services Canada (PWGSC), continued:

> "I don't think we have a backlog anymore, but I could be wrong…we are also dealing with what I would call the deeper root cause of this, in pursuing with the minister a so-called *pay modernization* approach. We're trying to invest or get support for investments into our backroom systems, which are very old, 40 years old. We're trying to get an investment so that we can optimize our system with off-the-shelf technology, and that would address the root cause."[21]

Again, dear reader, I will withhold my analysis for future chapters. But let us notice:

- There was no remaining backlog of payroll errors.
- The earlier problems were addressed entirely with human effort and better coordination.
- "Pay modernization" work was underway (we will learn more of this soon).

---

[21] Canada. Parliament. House of Commons. Standing Committee on Government Operations and Estimates. "Evidence." (n.d.), 39th Parliament, 2nd Session, Meeting 7. https://www.ourcommons.ca/DocumentViewer/en/39-2/OGGO/meeting-7/evidence, https://archive.is/QBBsw.

- Systems were "40 years old".
- An expression of hope was made for "off-the-shelf technology".
- No mention was made of modernizing/simplifying the collective agreements (e.g., 70,000+ regulations).

***

Two days later, December 12, the same committee heard from high-ranking witnesses. They talked past each other for a full two hours and a bias toward a *centralized* "off-the-shelf" technology was further imprinted into the minds of committee members.

The witnesses reiterated there was no longer an outstanding backlog of errors. 190,000 employees routinely received accurate paycheques in a timely manner. Exceptions were extremely rare and isolated.

Monique Boudrias, EVP of Canada Public Service Agency (CPSA), explained the root cause of said problems was the "[1] complexity of collective agreements and the web of rules; [2] the difference in business processes from department to department;

and [3] antiquated technology which causes duplication of data entry by departments"[22].

The committee learned that, in addition to experienced staff working overtime, "greater automation" had been employed. Diane Lorenzato, Assistant Deputy Minister with PWGSC, explained their efforts to "strengthen and modernize our compensation services continue unabated."

It is important to notice how some witnesses claimed the digital tools were "40 years old" while others provided hints that continuous evolution and improvement of digital systems was indeed happening.

Gilles Carpentier, a VP with CPSA, provided more context about their continuous improvement efforts. He told about a tool called "pay interface": an "electronic bridge automatically transferring pay data from existing departmental systems to PWGSC's central pay system".

Then — and this is momentous, so take a breath and refocus — Renée Jolicoeur, another Assistant Deputy

---

[22] Canada. Parliament. House of Commons. Standing Committee on Government Operations and Estimates. "Evidence." (n.d.), 39th Parliament, 2nd Session, Meeting 8. https://www.ourcommons.ca/DocumentViewer/en/39-2/OGGO/meeting-8/evidence, https://archive.is/FtTfJ.

Minister with PWGSC, shared details with the committee of two "major projects" in her department:

> "...a few years ago, PWGSC started to work on two major projects: *pension transformation* and *pay modernization*. Both projects consist of the replacement of IT systems...The pension project also includes the transfer of pension services to employees from departments to PWGSC, in fact to Shediac, New Brunswick.

> The pension project is fairly advanced. Most components will be in production in 2010...The pay modernization project has not started yet. It...will increase the automation exponentially."

Let us notice her sneaky, bureaucratic trick: she started by declaring "two" projects were started "a few years ago". And only after planting that seed did she then say, "the pay modernization project has not started yet."

One project had started. Not two.

Her trick was meant to protect a budget line item. Somewhere on a spreadsheet was the phrase "pay modernization" followed by a very large number, and her careful phraseology helped ensure said budget would remain earmarked for future. Clever.

Her description of those two projects was coloured with hopeful/impossible promises: employees, she said, would have "access to pension experts within seconds". And compensation advisers would have "time to provide advice to employees rather than spending their time inputting transactions in the system".

Phrases like those create a compelling story of a futuristic, quite supernatural system. Again, clever.

But which is it? Were there errors to be fixed or not? Were the current digital tools undergoing continual evolution and were they (nearly) fit-for-purpose? Or was a brand new, centralized, "off-the-shelf" system needed?

Perhaps the air in Ottawa causes MPs and bureaucrats to hallucinate; or is it the drinking water that makes them allergic to the facts right in front of their faces? I will draw your attention to another exchange between Daryl Kramp, Member of Parliament, and Renée Jolicoeur (paraphrased):

Daryl Kramp:

"...we have some new IT systems or payroll service systems coming online. I'm curious about two points on those. Is this a self-created or a designed set of software, or have you been able to, *per se*, buy this off the rack and use an existing program? Are we spending huge amounts of money for design or are we able to pick up something that's universally acceptable?"

Renée Jolicoeur:

"We are going to use what we call commercial off-the-shelf systems. These systems are already programmed. They are used by large corporations. In fact, before deciding on the models of service delivery that we will adopt, we consulted with large corporations, with other public services at the provincial and municipal levels. We are part of a number of benchmarking groups. Everybody is going in that direction now[23].

So, the model we will be using in government in a few years — because it takes time to implement those systems — is exactly the model used by the other public services presently or what will be used in the future. They are doing the same thing as we

---

[23] This may be a reference to the IBM report: "Pay Benchmarking Study". (See previous section.) Renée would have been aware, if not the sponsor, of the IBM report.

are. They are migrating to this more modern set-up for those functions."

Daryl Kramp:

"Personally, quite frankly, I'm pleased to hear that. I've had some experience with designer systems. The exponential cost of them is just unbelievable. So, I commend you on your decisions to go with a system with a proven track record and apply it to the government purposes."

What did Kramp mean by "proven track record"? Jolicoeur had, just seconds before, told him other public services were "migrating to this more modern set-up". Migrating, not migrated — she gave no evidence that any similar enterprise had successfully achieved such a migration.

He did not press for evidence from her and he was quick to ignore all the facts he heard in the first hour of the meeting: [1] the backlog of errors was resolved; [2] all 190,000 employees were getting paycheques routinely and without mistake; [3] the problems were caused by unchecked complexity of payroll rules (72 collective bargaining agreements and 70,000+ regulations); and [4] modernization of the existing systems (largely praised and deemed successful) continued "unabated".

Nonetheless and despite the data before them, appeal grew of an entirely new, centralized, modern, expensive, "off-the-shelf" system.

2008, February

Parliamentarians of the OGGO committee would hear from Diane Melançon again on February 5, 2008[24]:

> "Technology provides tools that can streamline our work, but in no way can it address 70,000 rules and regulations coming from legislation, Treasury Board, unions, *etc*... There is no easy button in compensation benefits."

And later in the meeting:

> "I have been working at Statistics Canada...There are four of us helping them out. It is just chaos over there...they're so backlogged it is unbelievable. We

---

[24] Canada. Parliament. House of Commons. Standing Committee on Government Operations and Estimates. "Evidence." (n.d.), 39th Parliament, 2nd Session, Meeting 10. https://www.ourcommons.ca/DocumentViewer/en/39-2/OGGO/meeting-10/evidence, https://archive.is/DmcWQ.

are still answering e-mails that employees have sent to the compensation unit going back to 2006.

...they're losing fully trained compensation advisers who are going to agencies that pay more for the same type of work."

And she added, in response to a subsequent question:

"They've begun to develop things so that employees in every department have access to their pay stubs, which they can print themselves...Employees currently do not have access to this system in all the departments. That's coming soon.

On December 12 [2007], they talked a lot about systems and change, but they indicated that they were still studying this and that it would be ready in three, five or 10 years. They're examining things, but we can't wait five or 10 years. The problem is here now."

My dear reader, Melançon was speaking from direct experience having been in the eye of the storm. Her anecdotes are important to our analysis of the Phoenix catastrophe for at least these two reasons.

First, because her testimony invokes difficult emotions in us all. Having just read her comments, you may feel anxious for her and for the plight of her colleagues. Naturally.

Second, because her passionate, first-hand stories can make us forget that the payroll apparatus was failing at a rate of only ~1%. Sure, 1% of a very large number of paycheques is a very large number of errors. Let's not deny there was a problem — but let's never presume that a replacement system, merely because it is newer and more centralized, will operate at a higher rate of success.

The Harper Era, 2nd Term

In autumn 2008, Canada's government took a brief intermission to hold an election.

Recall the election in 2006 resulted in a minority government for Harper's Conservative party. So, Harper rolled the dice by going back to the polls. It was a gamble that paid off — *sort of*. The Conservative party did not win a majority, as they hoped, but gained a few more seats.

***

Alicia Keys had *No One*, Katy Perry was *Hot N Cold*, and Lil Wayne made *A Milli* — actually, he made a few milli! Van Halen wrapped up a tour with David Lee Roth. And The Tragically Hip was enjoying some down time in their hometown of Kingston.

***

When Members of Parliament returned to Ottawa after the election, it must have felt they were returning from an intermission. Most of the committees and the business of the previous day continued. It was in *this* term that bureaucrats would develop faith in Phoenix.

Parliamentarians and bureaucrats would have heard frequent and fancy buzzwords from lobbyists and IT sales reps— let us recall the IT technology fads of the day:

- Turn-key systems
- CMS: Content Management Systems
- COTS: Commercial Off The Shelf systems
- Plug-n-play
- Intranet, Drupal, SharePoint
- Software-as-a-Service
- Social media

The future of IT looked bright and more promising than ever — large scale web services were becoming commonplace. Possibilities seemed endless and miraculous.

And so, Phoenix became an elixir, a panacea, a silver bullet. You will notice a mythology form in the minds of the elected Members of Parliament and senior public servants.

A Phoenix, after all, is unreal. Surreal. It is a myth. A bird that is said to have the ability to be reborn from its own ashes. It can regenerate and come back to life.

How could grown adults, particularly those who had achieved trusted positions in Canada's government, be so swept away by wishful thinking? I won't suggest they honestly believed that such a mythical creature exists; rather, they *behaved* as though such wishes could come true.

You will see they were willing — without evidence to support their position (i.e., faith) — to bet hundreds-of-millions of dollars *and* their jobs *and* political reputations that their Phoenix would rise.

***

Myths evolve through storytelling and cultural adaptation.

Consider the myth of the Greek goddess, Persephone. In the earliest stories, she was known as a goddess of vegetation and fertility —the myth began as an explanation of plant growth. But a curious, skeptical child must have asked, "why don't the plants grow in winter?" So, the story was adapted to include Persephone's abduction by Hades, the god of the underworld, and her eventual return to the world above with her mother Demeter. We can imagine a father talking to his child, "the plants don't grow in winter because Persephone is taken by Hades. Then she returns in the Spring with her mother." The myth became an explanation of the changing seasons.

With each meeting in Parliament, more stories were told of technological dysfunction and human suffering. (Yes, *suffering*. Perhaps to this book's detriment but with an eye to focus the topic, I have chosen to not go into detail about the human rights complaints [plural!] submitted these past few decades by compensation advisors and adjudicated by Canada's Human Rights Commission.) *Suffering indeed*.

With each story, the committee's witnesses and the Members of Parliament would adapt the evolving myth for their own context. "Some of my constituents are compensation advisors", an MP might think to themselves. "I too get frustrated with old software on my computer", a witness may empathize.

Myths become increasingly elaborate and their believers increasingly hyperbolic. If a story is told that contradicts the predominant narrative, the believers will adapt their myth to explain the contradiction.

2009, February

For example, at the Standing Committee on Finance (FINA) on February 10, 2009, parliamentarians were told this by MP Jean-Yves Laforest[25]:

> "...the Shawinigan Tax Centre is located in my riding. Employees at the centre...some are waiting as much as 12 weeks before collecting a paycheque. This problem dates back to last year when compensation services were centralized...

> Have you thought of a way to resolve this dilemma? Do you intend to revert to the old system where compensation services were decentralized? ...the situation is ridiculous."

---

[25] Canada. Parliament. House of Commons. Standing Committee on Finance. "Evidence." (n.d.), 40th Parliament, 2nd Session, Meeting 4. https://www.ourcommons.ca/DocumentViewer/en/40-2/FINA/meeting-4/evidence, https://archive.is/YyExH.

(I would not think less of you, my dear reader, if you missed that little detail. But I will repeat it for posterity's sake.)

Remember (in a previous chapter, I told you that) Renée Jolicoeur reported to Parliament that the centralization of payroll staff was the *solution* to their woes; but MP LaForest had just asserted that centralization of payroll staff was the *cause* of their woes.

Rather than add credence to the idea that a centralized system is *not* a magic bullet, bureaucrats would imagine their Phoenix with even *more* power.

In the transcripts of meetings in this period, many such contradictions are found. And with each passing day, the mythology grew more resilient.

What about dealing with RCMP superannuation? *Yes, the system will do that too — just the click of a button.*

We are modernizing the procurement process for large projects. *Yes, the new payroll project will use the most modern procurement techniques.*

We are seeing high staff turnover throughout the public service. *Yes, the payroll system will increase employee satisfaction and staff attrition will be reduced.*

We have payroll staff in many departments across the country. *Yes, the new payroll system will bring everyone together in one office.*

Every challenge would expand the solution. Like the myth of Hydra: the many-headed monster — if one of its heads was cut off, two more would grow back in its place.

Like Hydra, the promise of a centralized, off-the-shelf solution could not be slayed. Every piece of evidence that may weaken the idea was met with multiple arguments to strengthen it.

The *"payroll delivery system modernization project"* would soon take on its new name and a life of its own.

2009, Spring[26]

By this time, a few stars aligned that would commit the Canadian taxpayers to spending $300 million.

---

[26] Lessons learned from the Transformation of Pay Administration Initiative; Treasury Board of Canada Secretariat;https://www.canada.ca/en/treasury-board-secretariat/corporate/reports/lessons-learned-transformation-pay-administration-initiative.html, https://archive.is/Ldoai.

The PWGSC executives had kept their dreams alive (since ~1997) to rebuild all payroll and pension operations with a centralized system. Their plans were once again getting favourable attention from the government of the day.

With some success (e.g., nothing blew up and the sky didn't fall), the public works department oversaw the production of new software systems for *pension* administration and relocated those jobs to a central location. It was argued the same could now be done for *payroll.*

A business case produced by PWGSC calculated ~1,400 jobs scattered across the country could be replaced by only ~550 *if* the payroll operation was centralized. They estimated a savings of $70 million per year.

Figure 1: Photo of Business Case document, 2009. Photo published by CBC, 2017.

Behind the scenes, there were rumblings that all IT staff would be restructured. It was evident that executives of the day had "centralization" on their minds. "Shared Services", we might say, was *all the rage*. (Watch for, in the following pages, the official creation of a new department called "Shared Services Canada".)

And the smartphone craze had begun. iPhone, Droid, Blackberry — these devices were mainstream, and the possibilities seemed limitless. People were using apps daily such as Facebook and Twitter — sites that reached billions of users. The government's payroll systems never looked more archaic. It must have seemed, to MPs and executives alike, that their IT systems were cobbled together by lesser humans. Certainly, the mood to "modernize" had never been stronger.

And so it was, Parliament got behind the plan to centralize the payroll operations into a single office with a new, off-the-shelf software system.

2009, July

In support of the business case, Cabinet approved $123 million for business process changes (to centralize the office); and $186 million for IT systems development.

Oracle's *PeopleSoft*, it was decided, would be the core technology of the new systems.

Why PeopleSoft? Because it was already in use by HR departments throughout Canada's government. PeopleSoft was the core technology in a system called "GCHR" (Government of Canada Human Resources). It was thought, by proponents of the Phoenix project, that standardizing on PeopleSoft would easily enable the development/integration of new requirements.

Reports, years later, would tell of "hundreds of pages" of requirements.

2010, February

An RFP was issued by Public Services and Procurement Canada (PSPC). They sought proposals from companies with prior experience integrating Oracle's PeopleSoft.

2010, March

A contract was issued to ADGA, a staffing agency, for Project Management services. However, rather than contract ADGA to manage the project, they merely provided staff to the PSPC bureaucrats who maintained they could manage the project themselves.

I tell you this because this was criticized in a formal review of the project *years later*. The Treasury Board would eventually conclude that PSPC "did not have the necessary capacity and/or capability to carry out their responsibilities"[27].

---

[27] Lessons learned from the Transformation of Pay Administration Initiative; Treasury Board of Canada Secretariat; https://www.canada.ca/en/treasury-board-secretariat/corporate/reports/lessons-learned-transformation-pay-administration-initiative.html, https://archive.is/Ldoai.

2010, August

Stephen Harper announced payroll activities would be centralized in a new "Pay Centre" in Miramichi, New Brunswick.

This relates to our little book for two reasons:

First, Harper's announcement indicated a timeline for the Pay Centre that was 9 months later than anticipated by the managers responsible for the Phoenix project. Hence, project managers *declared* the training of ~550 employees at the new Pay Centre would be delayed.

Whether that claim was true cannot be known: Are we to believe the project was, in all other aspects, going perfectly to schedule?

Second, why Miramichi? Is this where Canada's payroll experts are found? Is there something in the local water that improves math and finance skills?

Miramichi was a political wedge. Harper vowed to end the "Long Gun Registry" — doing so was popular among rural voters, First Nations, hunters, *etc.* But the move was criticized because the Firearms Centre in Miramichi was a large employer in the region. Harper saw an opportunity to combine these policies: if the Pay

Centre was to be centralized and the Firearms Centre was to be downsized, then Miramichi was both practically and politically convenient.

The Harper Era, 3rd Term

In early 2011, Harper called an election. Again, the gamble paid off — his Conservative party won a majority and an increase in the popular vote.

***

Bruno Mars threw a *Grenade*. Katy Perry launched *Fireworks*. Taio Cruz went on and on, he told us once, he told us twice, then lit it up with *Dynamite*. Meanwhile, Susan Boyle had *The Gift* and Foo Fighters were *Wasting Light*. Van Halen and The Tragically Hip were both in studio recording new albums.

***

It is not clear (to me, as I have found no publicly available evidence) whether the project was called "Phoenix" at this time. No matter what it was called, it had grown wings and was in flight.

From this point forward, it would gain momentum.

2011, June

"Pay Modernization" contracts were awarded to IBM and Oracle. The contracts described 8 years of activity.

2011, August

In a separate stream of policy making, Canada's government was working to establish a new department called Shared Services Canada (SSC). The launch of SSC was announced in August and the new department was to be responsible for the administration of all email, telecom, and data centres.

(Remember in an earlier chapter, I suggested you watch for this. Well, here it is. And this topic will return in upcoming pages.)

2011, December

Public Services began implementing the "pay-consolidation" portion of the project. Executives reported it would take 4 years to consolidate 56 departments into just one. ~1,400 personnel across Canada would be replaced by 550 in Miramichi.

2012, May

The new Pay Centre opened in Miramichi (in temporary office space) and the first 145 employees moved in.[28]

Claims were made in the official press release that taxpayers would enjoy $78 million in annual savings as early as 2016.

(Spoiler alert: Taxpayers would be deeply disappointed.)

2012, December

Consolidation (in Miramichi) of staff continued. And the bureaucrats in the Public Works department announced they would begin implementing the "pay modernization" portion of the project — the IT portion.

---

[28] Government of Canada opens its new pay centre in Miramichi, New Brunswick, Government of Canada, accessed 2012-05-28 https://www.canada.ca/en/news/archive/2012/05/government-canada-opens-its-new-pay-centre-miramichi-new-brunswick.html, https://archive.is/ZPRov.

2014, June

SSC (remember, they were responsible for the administration of data centres) were delayed in their work to produce a testing environment for the IBM and Oracle contractors. This delay, in the coming months, would add pressure to the already-complex testing effort.

Two other events in June are important to our story:

- Renée Jolicoeur retired. (Remember her?) She would later be described by journalists as an "architect" of the Phoenix project[29].
- PSPC announced that the *design* of the payroll system was "complete".

Declaring that the design is "complete" at precisely the moment its designer retired is curious. Is it not?

I don't mean to ascribe ill-will or malintent upon her or others — her retirement was pending and the status of this project would have factored into her decision. No

---

[29] Bagnall, J. (2018, February 24). Risks unheeded, journey without end: The seeds of the tortured Phoenix pay project were planted three decades ago. Ottawa Citizen. Retrieved March 2, 2023, from https://ottawacitizen.com/news/politics/risks-unheeded-journey-without-end-the-seeds-of-the-tortured-phoenix-pay-project-were-planted-three-decades-ago, https://archive.is/vK758.

doubt, she wanted to see the project achieve this important milestone. And upon announcing her retirement, her colleagues would of course remark and congratulate her for, among other things, her contribution to the design of new payroll systems.

This coincidence tells us very little about the *actual* status of the project but tells us volumes about the ever-evolving myth. Her retirement is a milestone we must analyse carefully.

"The designer retired", they would say. "The design is done", they would conclude. "It is good, it is right", they were inclined to believe. "It will save us all..." *etc.*

From there onward, changing the design would grow exponentially more difficult. This, I assert, for two reasons:

First, regardless of one's opinion or personal experience with Jolicoeur, her reputation would loom large. Her successors, when they would *necessarily* propose changes to the design, would compete against a powerful confirmation bias: the perceived correctness of her design was indisputable. (*Literally, she wouldn't be around to dispute it.*) Simultaneously, the *flaws* in her design were forever memorialized. She wasn't around to defend herself. To some, she would be the perfect scapegoat.

Consider: how hard would *you* fight to change the design or introduce new requirements? Fighting for a change would introduce serious personal consequences; and *not* fighting introduced *zero* personal consequences.

Second, as every project manager knows, an important set of gates will close when the design is announced "complete", and other important gates will open.

Need to change the design? Sorry, that door is now closed. (...or heavily guarded.) Need to spend another large batch of money? Congratulations, that door is now open.

Of course, you and I both know the design was not "complete" — this was 100% not true. History will show the design was deeply flawed. That, or (as certain bureaucrats will argue in the years that followed) the design was perfect but the *implementers* were to blame. Or the implementers were right and the users were to blame.

"We designed it right; they built it wrong", they would say. "We built it to spec; the design was wrong", others would say. "The design and implementation were right; but the staff weren't trained properly to use it", *etc.*

2015, March: Escape the Phoenix

My dear reader, I looked everywhere...I scoured the internet...I read every news article...I spent more hours than I care to admit searching the government's websites. I looked for the earliest use of the monicker, "Phoenix", so I could report to you who coined the term.

Up until this point in time, the project was called TPA (Transformation of Pay Administration Initiative).

The first use of the term that I could find in publicly available records is in the transcript of a meeting of the Standing Committee on National Defence (NDDN) on March 11, 2015.[30]

This is also the first evidence I found that some government departments wanted nothing to do with it!

---

[30] Parliament of Canada. "Evidence - NDDN (41-2) - No. 51 - House of Commons of Canada." URL: https://www.ourcommons.ca/DocumentViewer/en/41-2/NDDN/meeting-51/evidence. Accessed on 02/03/2023, https://archive.is/26RWP. Accessed on 2023-03-21.

MP Julian Fantino, in an otherwise unrelated conversation about military funding, said:

> "For personal security reasons, CSE (Communications Security Establishment) has chosen to continue to administer the pay of its employees independently of other departments. This means that it has opted out of integrating with the government-wide Phoenix pay system..."

MP Cheryl Gallant responded with surprise or perhaps concern: "Are they implying, though, that the payroll in general is subject to breaches?"

Fantino answered her question by repeating that the nature of CSE's work demands secrecy and the protection of personnel records[31].

Gallant's concern was warranted — just months later, Canadians would learn about the first of many privacy breaches whereby confidential employee data were exposed.

---

[31] Committee Proceedings - NDDN (41-2) - March 11, 2015 -Part 2, Parlvu, accessed 2023-03-21, https://parlvu.parl.gc.ca/Harmony/en/PowerBrowser/PowerBrowserV 2/20150311/- 1/14235?Embedded=true&globalstreamId=20&startposition=4927&vie wMode=3

Concurrently, in other committees, test plans were changing by the day. Earlier test plans called for a "pilot" rollout of Phoenix in the Natural Resources department. The idea was to perform payroll in both the old and new systems simultaneously then reconcile one against the other. The new plan was to pilot the software only within Public Works — the department managing the project.

If you experienced a sudden loss of confidence in the quality of the new system upon hearing that the project managers didn't want an outside department to see the test results, you wouldn't be the first.

Prepare for more news like this — *it's going to get much worse!*

2015, April

With the certainty of an election within the year, all federal party leaders were in campaign mode. Stephen Harper visited Miramichi to reiterate the plan for their community[32]. He indicated Phoenix would go online by December and a new Pay Centre building would be ready by 2018. The 550 jobs promised in the plan were already filled and the new payroll employees were occupying temporary offices.

2015, July

"Highly sensitive" data for 10,000 public servants was leaked to IBM's servers[33]. This was the earliest reported case of a privacy breach related to Phoenix. Others followed.

With pressure building toward unrealistic, pre-determined release dates, we can be certain there were arguments about the feasibility and scope of a December launch. For example, the plans called for an adjustment to the software that would enable the calculation and display of numbers with 3 decimal points instead of just 2 (does that seem important to

---

[32] CBC News, "Harper announces contract for Miramichi pay centre," CBC News, April 10, 2015, https://www.cbc.ca/news/canada/new-brunswick/harper-announces-contract-for-miramichi-pay-centre-1.3020212, https://archive.is/9C8kU.

[33] CBC News, "Phoenix privacy breach highlights need for independent oversight of government," CBC News, last modified July 12, 2016, https://www.cbc.ca/news/politics/phoenix-privacy-breach-wier-cavoukian-1.3691866, https://archive.is/NAJul.

you?) — this requirement (among others) was dropped from the December deadline.

2015, September

Right on schedule, the relevant departments received a "readiness checklist" for Phoenix.

But...was Phoenix itself ready? *No!*

And as luck would have it, someone got that message through to the stubborn bureaucrats and politicians. Reluctantly, to be sure, they accepted that a December launch was impossible. (To be precise, the initial rollout was to be in two stages: first in October, then December.)

New promises were made:

- "Testing" (whatever that means) was moved to January 2016.
- And the two-stage rollout was moved to February (34 departments with 120,000 employees) and April (67 departments with 170,000 employees).

Interlude

In autumn, 2015, Canadians went back to the polls to elect their next government. And before we continue our chronological review, let us dedicate a few pages to understand the conditions of the Phoenix project at that point in time.

What were the conditions the next government would inherit? And why did they *not* stop the derailment when they had the chance?

We know, with hindsight, the decision to launch Phoenix was an unimaginably bad idea. But the question we must soon ask ourselves, and the true purpose of this little book, is whether sufficient information was available to disconfirm their plans and cause them to take a different course of action.

Could the catastrophe have been avoided? And should they have known better?

I believe so.

Current Condition

- 26 years had passed since 1989 when Brian Mulroney's government undertook a study to modernize compensation administration systems.

- *Hundreds of millions of paycheques had been accurately calculated and successfully delivered to federal employees in those 26 years.*

- True, the "old system" was capable of errors. Brigitte Fortin, Assistant Deputy Minister at PWGSC reported that "at the time we went live" with Phoenix there were 18,000 outstanding cases of overpayments with a combined amount of $21.7 million.[34]

- Employee attrition was high among compensation advisors; this was attributed primarily to the growing complexity of the work due to 72+ collective agreements.

- Five Prime Ministers had held office: Mulroney, Campbell, Chrétien, Martin, Harper.

---

[34] House of Commons. (n.d.). Meeting No. 25 - Standing Committee on Government Operations and Estimates. Evidence [Transcript]. Parliament of Canada. https://www.ourcommons.ca/DocumentViewer/en/42-1/OGGO/meeting-25/evidence#Int-9030239, https://archive.is/TXwlN.

- $354 million (at minimum) had been spent: $45 million to Accenture, plus an unknown legal settlement, plus $123 million to establish offices in Miramichi, plus $186 million for the development of Phoenix software systems.
- 290,000 federal employees across 101 departments were to be paid through Phoenix. (Recall the study in 1989 included only 186,000.)
- It's unclear how many compensation advisors were on staff at this time: recall there were ~1,400 before 550 new positions were established in Miramichi. (Some evidence suggests there were 550 employees in Miramichi and still 790 in other locations.)
- One Security breach had already been reported.
- Six years since project approval: July 2009.
- 4.5 years since first contracts awarded to ADGA: March 2010.
- Four years since development contracts awarded to IBM and Oracle: June 2011.
- One year since Phoenix's design was declared "complete": June 2014.

"Official" Project Status

To learn the "actual" project status (the truth), we will continue our chronological review following this chapter. For now, let us look instead at the "official" status — what did bureaucrats *say* was true?

The administrators of the Phoenix project indicated they had reached a phase called "Execution/Construction" and were nearing a condition they called "Deployment Readiness".

Summary Of The Project Plan

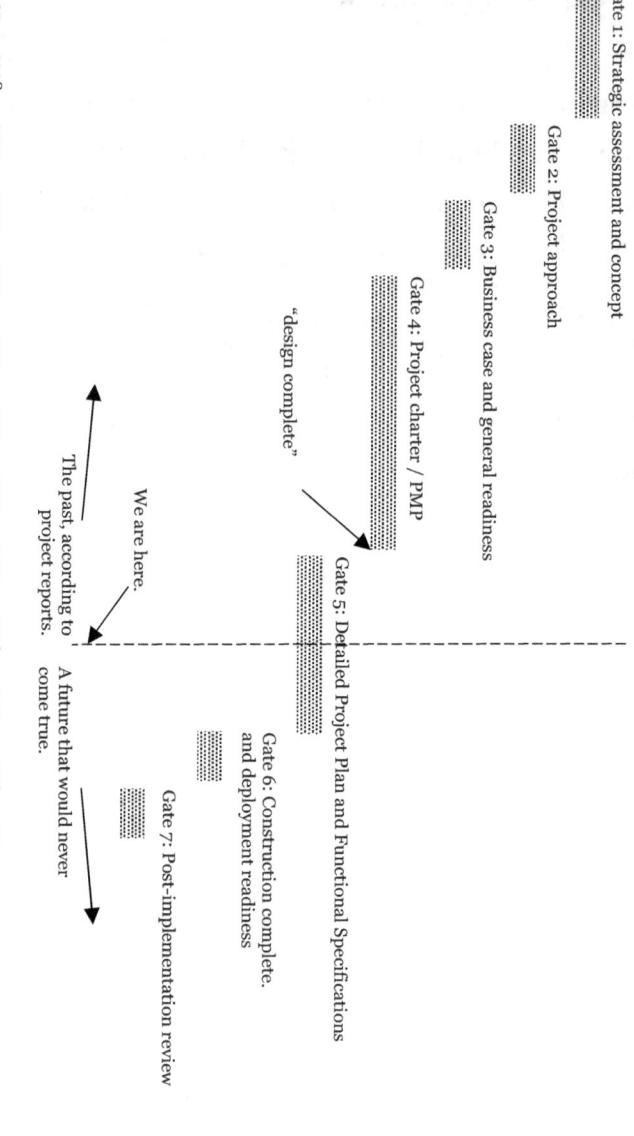

| 2007 | 2008 | 2009 | 2010 | 2011 | 2012 | 0213 | 2014 | 2015 | 2016 | 2017 | 2018 | 2019 | 2020 | 2021 | 2022 | 2023 |

Gate 1: Strategic assessment and concept

Gate 2: Project approach

Gate 3: Business case and general readiness

Gate 4: Project charter / PMP

"design complete"

Gate 5: Detailed Project Plan and Functional Specifications

We are here.

The past, according to project reports.

A future that would never come true.

Gate 6: Construction complete, and deployment readiness

Gate 7: Post-implementation review

What does "Deployment Readiness" mean?

Canada's Treasury Board published *A Guide to Project Gating for IT-Enabled Projects* in 2010[35]. It was a handbook for project managers. It described how funding was governed by the Treasury Board.

With cryptic acronyms and the language of officialdom, the document prescribed a non-negotiable sequence of project "gates". As each gate is (supposedly) passed, additional funding may be released. *(See diagram on next page.)*

When managing a large software project for Canada's federal government, was it more important to serve the needs of the Treasury Board than to serve the needs of end users?

If you don't give users what they need, they merely submit complaints; but if you don't give Treasury Board what they need, they will withhold money.

Conversely: if you give users what they need, perhaps you get a smile and a "thanks"; but if you give Treasury Board what they need, perhaps you get a bonus.

---

[35] Treasury Board of Canada Secretariat, Information Management: A Common Approach, accessed March 3, 2023, https://www.tbs-sct.canada.ca/itp-pti/pog-spg/irp-gpgitep/irp-gpgitep-eng.pdf, https://archive.is/IM44m.

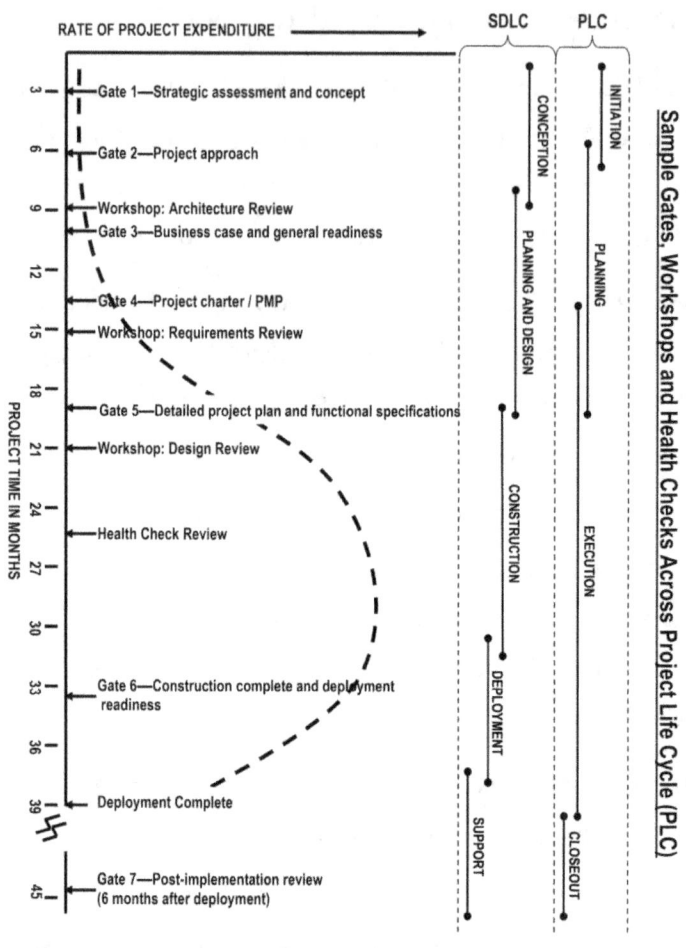

Figure 2: Example Project Expenditure Governance Diagram, page 27, Treasury Board of Canada Secretariat, Information Management: A Common Approach

This document means: if your project complies with this model, your project will be *funded* and your bonus will be granted. It does *not* mean your project will be *successful*.

Strangely, and against all evidence, project managers continued (and continue!) to believe that adherence to the gates prescribed by Treasury Board ensures *success* of their project.

This is wishful thinking. Superstition. *Myth*.

The Waterfall Myth

The Treasury Board declared in the document on page 27, "the SDLC (Systems Delivery Life Cycle) follows a *traditional waterfall*".

Consider our recent study of the Phoenix myth and how it evolved in the minds of executives and administrators. You are well equipped to imagine how myths can propagate in the world of IT management. And there are few myths more potent than the "traditional waterfall".

***

My dear reader, I did not intend to write a book to brood about the Waterfall myth — but an excursion into the topic is required because Canada's Treasury

Board declared that all funding for IT projects is governed by this mysterious doctrine. The Treasury Board's adherence to the Waterfall is, in many ways, *the cause* of the Phoenix catastrophe — the project was doomed from the start.

For some of my readers, that goes without saying; for others, a fulsome explanation is needed. I would fail in my duty, as your loyal guide and historian, to presume you know what a "traditional waterfall" is. And it would be unfair of me to presume you are aware of the technical literature and empirical data showing its low efficacy relative to other techniques.

You may have questions:

- What is the "traditional waterfall"?
- Is it the best way to govern IT projects?
- What impact does this have on the quality of software?
- Could Canada's Treasury govern their funding by other means?

The remainder of this chapter is dedicated to answering these questions, and more.

I will tell you a little about the Waterfall myth, its history and prevalence. I will also tell you that many IT teams have abandoned the concept and I will share some of the alternatives they have devised. We will review the seminal texts, historical figures, and key concepts related to "The Waterfall" and a competing set of ideas, "Agile".

My goal, to serve you – my reader, is that you will understand the divergence, the giant chasm between project management patterns of Canada's government versus the patterns used by modern IT organizations.

(If you know the answers to such questions and are familiar with Waterfall, Agile, and the like, please skim or skip to the next chapter.)

***

So, on with it then...

On the topic of the "traditional waterfall", there is nothing "traditional" about it. It is not a holiday or a song; it is not a technique passed through the generations like cuisine or hunting.

The Waterfall is a *convention* invented by consultants, adopted by bureaucracies — it is a fiscal habit enforced by fiat and it *never* made sense applied to IT systems development.

And always remember, a waterfall is a giant cliff!

***

All myths begin as stories that explain difficult questions. The Waterfall myth began when someone asked: "How shall we *build* large IT systems?"

Humans have a long history of building things: roads, bridges, aqueducts, pyramids, houses, cars, airplanes, skyscrapers.

Such projects have insurmountable technical dependencies. When building a bridge, the foundation and piers must be in place to support the weight of the bridge, the deck, and the loads it will carry — the laws of gravity require that we install those components in a precise sequence. When assembling a car, the cab must exist before it can be attached to the chassis, and wheels must be installed before the vehicle can roll.

These technical dependencies create what project managers have long called "a critical path": a non-negotiable sequence from start to finish. You may have heard of a Gantt Chart? Henry Gantt popularized the technique to illustrate the critical path of a project[36].

When a critical path dependency graph is illustrated, it produces a sequence of descending steps — coined "The Waterfall".

Early in the digital era, when enterprises were grappling with the new challenges of IT development, they had such metaphors in mind: building bridges, assembling cars, mass production lines.

Due to technical dependency, these activities tend to follow a common pattern:

Plan ↘

    Design ↘

        Build ↘

            Test ↘

                Operate/Maintain

So, the same phases/gates were applied to digital system development and ill-informed managers believed the ill-conceived notion that project work must pass from one step to the next, like a baton in a relay race.

---

[36] "Gantt chart," Wikipedia, accessed March 2, 2023, https://en.wikipedia.org/wiki/Gantt_chart

Notice, and this is important but easily ignored, believing a critical path exists requires the pre-supposition that the end state can be known. In other words, if you believe that there is a critical path, you must also presume that the desired outcome is fixed and can be precisely defined *before* the project begins.

Consider house construction, for example. Before a shovel ever touches dirt, we can model the house in near-perfect detail. Blueprints indicate precise positioning of load-bearing posts, electrical components, water pipes, doors, windows. With 3D imaging, we can produce virtual "walk-throughs" of the house complete with paint, wallpapers, textured floors, and a TV playing in the living room. Before construction begins, we can predict the area of the roof and floors and pre-order the precise quantity of lumber, shingles, and carpets. The end state can be known in advance with a high degree of certainty.

This is *never* true in the realm of digital systems development. *Never!*

Anyone who believes the end state of an IT system can be known and that a critical path exists, has made a category error[37]. The metaphors they have playing in their minds are wrong: mass production, assembly, construction. When they ought to be thinking of experimentation, composition, innovation, creation.

When the most stubborn argue with me on this point, I simply ask: "Can the end state of the *source code* be known in advance?" Perhaps high-level requirements and business rules can be known in advance (e.g., you are building an e-commerce service and you can predict you will accept specific credit cards and apply specific regional taxes), but at the level of *source code* — the appropriate level of analysis — all bets are off. The argument is over. The end state cannot be known and there is no critical path.

Digital systems development is a creative activity. Sure, some patterns and reusable components are useful. But these are not snapped together like puzzle pieces. They are composed, uniquely, bespoke.

---

[37] A category error, also known as a category mistake, is a type of logical or semantic error that occurs when someone uses terms or concepts from one category or domain inappropriately in another category or domain.

Dr. Winston Royce

The Waterfall myth had already captured hearts and minds by the late 1960's.

In an essay published in 1970 called *Managing the Development of Large Software Systems*[38], Dr. Winston Royce expanded the myth significantly — though perhaps unintentionally.

The term "Waterfall" does not appear in the essay, but clearly he was critical of the concept. In the first few paragraphs and immediately following an illustration of a typical Waterfall, he argued it "is risky and invites failure".

In the remaining pages, he shared strategies to avoid known pitfalls. Among the strategies he described is a rather prophetic foreshadowing of a technique that would capture the mainstream decades later: *iterate!*

Specifically, he said "do the job twice if possible" — the first iteration should be brief (roughly 1/3rd the estimated timeline) but comprehensive enough to "test

---

[38] Winston Royce, "Managing The Development Of Large Software Systems," in Proceedings of IEEE WESCON, August 1970, 1-9.

key hypotheses", and "sense the trouble spots in the design, model them, and model their alternatives".

Brilliant!

But his essay also, unfortunately, reinforced key elements of the Waterfall myth:

- Royce argued "begin the design process with program designers, *not* analysts and programmers".
- And "ensure that a preliminary program design is complete *before* analysis begins".

To understand the context of those suggestions, and to understand why Royce had not yet abandoned the Waterfall myth entirely, it helps to remember that computers were the size of trucks and the cost of change was extremely high. A design flaw discovered late in development was expensive and time-consuming: much more than changing a few lines of code, imagine having to disassemble a truck-size computer, manufacture new components, and rewire entire electrical circuits.

I believe Royce had *not* made the category error I described earlier — he did *not* (I believe) think that the end state of a software system could be known in advance. Rather, I believe he accepted that the end state is impossible to know, but he pragmatically calculated the extreme cost of *change* late in development (given contemporary technology).

So, it therefore made sense to Royce and his contemporaries to spend the requisite time designing with chalkboard and paper before employing analysts and programmers (i.e., the people who assembled the hardware, operated the keypunch machines, catalogued the punch cards, and ran the programs).

These days, hardware components are standardized; architectural components are virtualized; and the average Bluetooth earbud can receive over-the-air firmware updates and has a *million* times more computing power than the Apollo spacecraft. Changing a program late in development incurs *trivial* cost — yet the segregation Royce advised persists in many IT organizations.

IBM & Fred Brooks

IBM's influence across the industry cannot be overstated. IBM has long been a primary contractor to governments around the world. Their methods have dominated project management practices, business administration, and university curricula for a century.

And through that period, IBM's development process has emphasized a sequenced/gated approach that segregates activities and people by skill and authority (i.e., the Waterfall):

- Authoritative decision makers determine budget, scope, architecture, before...
- Less authoritative employees gather detailed requirements and produce design documents, before...
- Less authoritative implementers use said design documents to produce usable functionality, before...
- Even less authoritative testers are granted access to the near-complete system, before...
- The system is finally released to end users.

That is the "IBM Method" or the "Systems Development Life Cycle (SDLC)". It evolved through the years and would later be known as "Object-Oriented Software Process (OOSP)", then "Rational Unified Process (RUP)". With each new acronym, IBM would update minor details but they have never abandoned the fundamental feature of the Waterfall: a gated sequence of segregated activities.

Canada's government, as they expanded their IT infrastructure through the 1960's and 70's, acquired more than IBM's hardware — they also adopted IBM's project management methods. And to understand the prevailing management techniques at IBM at the time, we can study a book published in 1975, *The Mythical Man Month*, by Frederick Brooks.

Brooks is renowned for his involvement as development manager of the IBM OS/360 system. (He also famously wrote "Adding manpower to a late software project makes it later".)

Like Royce before him, Brooks favoured (reasonable) segregation of design from development (*circa* 1975). He wrote, for example, "the system must have conceptual integrity, which can only be achieved by separating architecture from implementation"[39]. Given the era and the high cost of computer hardware at the time, I think the advice was warranted. Unfortunately, many project managers and consultants took that

---

[39] Brooks, F. P. Jr. The Mythical Man Month, Anniversary edition with 4 new chapters, Addison-Wesley (1995), itself reprinted from the Proceedings of the IFIP Tenth World Computing Conference, H.-J. Kugler, ed., Elsevier Science B.V., Amsterdam, NL (1986) pp. 1068-76.

advice to justify the Waterfall in both the development of hardware *and* software.

But, (like Royce) Brooks had *not* made the category error described earlier — he did *not* favour the Waterfall in situations where the cost of change is low, and he warned against the tenets of Waterfall in at least two ways:

First, he dedicated whole essays warning his contemporaries there is *No Silver Bullet* — the allure of dogmas must be resisted.

Second, (in the 1995 reprint of *The Mythical Man Month*) he explained that the best software is grown (incrementally), not built:

> "I still remember the jolt I felt in 1958 when I first heard a friend talk about *building* a program, as opposed to *writing* one...
>
> The building metaphor has outlived its usefulness. It is time to change again...any software system should be grown by incremental development...I have seen the most dramatic results since I began urging this technique...nothing in the past decade has so radically changed my own practice, or its

effectiveness...teams can *grow* much more complex entities in four months than they can *build*."

NASA & US Department of Defence

By the mid-1980's, the United States Department of Defence published a standard operating procedure for the procurement and development of digital systems. It was called DoD-Std-2167, also known as "Defense System Software Development". A revision was published 3 years later, DoD-Std-2167A.

Both documents expand the Waterfall myth in their own ways and were used extensively in the development of military software projects during the late 80's and early 90's.

However, the standard was criticized for being too prescriptive and not flexible enough to accommodate changes in software development practices.

To their credit — and this is *momentous* — those standard procedures were made obsolete in 1994 with the publication of MIL-STD-498 where this amazing paragraph is found:

"If the CDRL[40] lays out a strict 'Waterfall' sequence of deliverables, little room is left to propose innovative development processes. If the CDRL forces all CSCIs[41] into lock-step with each other, little room is left to develop the CSCIs in an optimum order. To the maximum extent possible, the CDRL should avoid such pre-determination, leaving the door open for incremental delivery of software products, staggered development of CSCIs, and other variations to optimize the software development effort."[42]

Wow!

To repeat: "...to the maximum extent possible...avoid [the Waterfall]", and instead leave "the door open for incremental delivery".

And they really meant it. Nowhere in the document is a diagram that resembles a Gantt chart. Instead, the document provides *flow*charts in various configurations with (and to prevent the reader

---

[40] Contract Data Requirements List
[41] Computer Software Configuration Items
[42] "Military Standard Software Development and Documentation" (Department of Defence Standard MIL-STD-498), accessed on DLA Quick Search website, https://quicksearch.dla.mil/Transient/32399B21A8724A84925D0FC2 B12FAE6B.pdf, https://archive.is/FNYbq.

mistaking the flowcharts for dependency graphs) comments like, "all activities may be more ongoing, overlapping, and iterative than the figure is able to show."

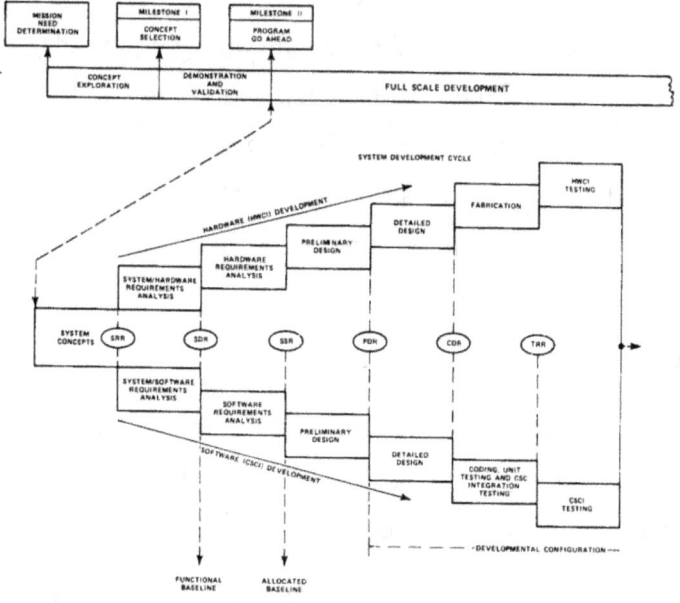

FIGURE 1. System development cycle within the system life cycle.

Figure 3: Process diagram from DoD-Std-2167, 1985

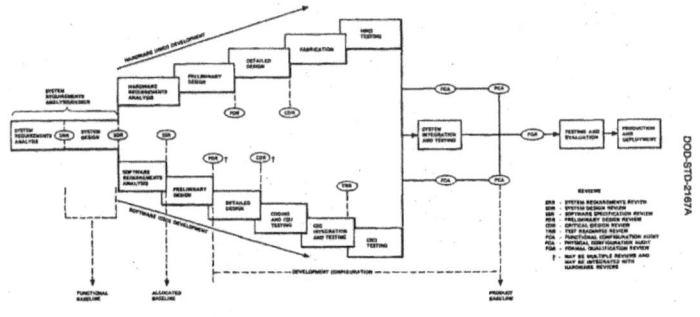

FIGURE 1. An example of system development reviews and audits.

Figure 4:Process diagram from DoD-Std-2167A, 1988

Included is a flowchart that describes the activities that may be undertaken to achieve the first build of a system, and under a box called "System Requirements Analysis" is an asterisk with the helpful note: "Preliminary/partial". (*Wow*, this implies the first build can begin without fully knowing the requirements.)

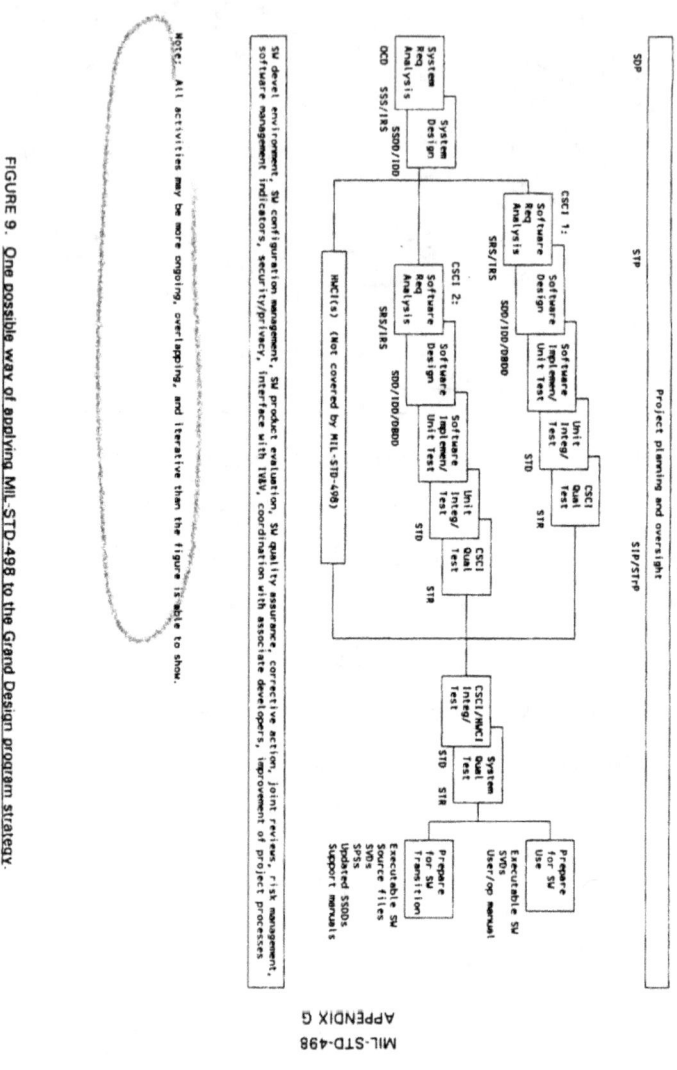

FIGURE 9. One possible way of applying MIL-STD-498 to the Grand Design program strategy.

MIL-STD-498
APPENDIX G

108

Figure 5: Example applying MIL-STD-498 to program strategy.

The working group even published a commentary[43] about MIL-STD-498 to provide further context and examples. I particularly enjoy a section called *Accommodating Incremental and Evolutionary Development* where they explain:

> "MIL-STD-498 is written in terms of developing software in *multiple* 'builds'. Each build incorporates a specified subset of the planned capabilities of the software. The builds might be prototypes, versions offering partial functionality, or other partial or complete versions of the software."

This document is a revolutionary departure from the Waterfall myth. Too bad Canada's government would lag decades behind.

---

[43] MIL-STD-498" Crosstalk: The Journal of Defense Software Engineering 8, no. 2 (February 1995). Accessed May 31, 2010. http://www.stsc.hill.af.mil/crosstalk/1995/02/MILSTD.asp, https://web.archive.org/web/20100531034813/http://www.stsc.hill.af.mil/crosstalk/1995/02/MILSTD.asp.

Activity	Builds			
	Build 1	Build 2	Build 3	Build 4
5.1 Project planning and oversight	X	X	X	X
5.2 Establishing a software development environment	X	X	X	X
5.3 System requirements analysis	X	X		
5.4 System design	X	X	X	
5.5 Software requirements analysis	X	X	X	X
5.6 Software design	X	X	X	X
5.7 Software implementation and unit testing	X	X	X	X
5.8 Unit integration and testing	X	X	X	X
5.9 CSCI qualification testing		X	X	X
5.10 CSCI/HWCI integration and testing		X	X	X
5.11 System qualification testing			X	X
5.12 Prepare for software use	X	X	X	X
5.13 Prepare for software transition				X
Integral processes:				
5.14 Software configuration management	X	X	X	X
5.15 Software product evaluation	X	X	X	X
5.16 Software quality assurance	X	X	X	X
5.17 Corrective action	X	X	X	X
5.18 Joint technical and management reviews	X	X	X	X
5.19 Other activities	X	X	X	X
Figure 2: One Possible Mapping of MIL-STD-498 Activities to Multiple Builds.				

Figure 6: Example incremental builds, MIL-STD-498 working group.

Hirotaka Takeuchi and Ikujiro Nonaka

Not everyone was entranced by the Waterfall myth.

In 1986, an essay appeared in Harvard Business Review called *The New New Product Development Game*[44].

Takeuchi and Nonaka pointed out evident failures of the Waterfall:

> "Under the sequential or relay race approach a project goes through several phases...moving from one phase to the next only after all the requirements of the preceding phase are satisfied...A bottleneck in one phase can slow or even halt the entire development process...

> ...the crucial problems tend to occur at the points where one group passes the project to the next."

They described an alternate approach wherein:

> "...the phases overlap considerably, which enables the group to absorb the vibration or 'noise' generated throughout the development process. When a bottleneck appears...the process does not come to a sudden halt; the team manages to push itself forward."

---

[44] Hirotaka Takeuchi and Ikujiro Nonaka, "The New New Product Development Game," Harvard Business Review 64, no. 1 (January-February 1986): 137-146.

The essay included case studies from Honda, 3M, NEC, Epson, Brother, Canon, Hewlett-Packard, and Fuji-Xerox. The authors noted six patterns of management observed in all cases:

- built-in instability
- self-organizing project teams
- overlapping development phases
- "multi-learning"
- subtle control
- organizational transfer of learning

These characteristics are not just different, but fundamentally at odds with the premises of the Waterfall: division of labour, sequential phases, authoritative control, *etc.*

Takeuchi and Nonaka emphasize that "product development seldom proceeds in a linear and static manner. It involves an iterative and dynamic process." The role of executives, they argue, is to set "challenging goals" and exert "subtle forms of control" while enabling self-organizing teams that act with high levels of autonomy.

Furthermore, executives must create an environment that tolerates "ambiguity" wherein everyone understands "operational decisions are made incrementally" and "important strategic decisions are delayed as much as possible in order to allow a more flexible response to last-minute feedback".

The essay also introduced a rugby metaphor. They mentioned "a holistic method — as in *rugby*, the ball gets passed within the team as it moves as a unit up the field". Extending the metaphor further, they incorporated a rugby term, "Scrum", and labelled an entire section of the essay, *Moving the Scrum Downfield*.

The ideas of Takeuchi's and Nonaka's essay were revolutionary and compelling. They were boldly writing about team-based work rather than divisions of labour. Even among their contemporaries on the cutting edge of the industry, it would take a decade and the ingenuity of others to adapt *The New New Product Development Game* into an actionable, pragmatic, repeatable framework for managing software projects. That framework would become known simply as *Scrum* (see next section).

***

My dear reader, you can be forgiven if you've read these recent paragraphs and are left thinking, "Rugby? Scrum? Self-organizing team? What does this have to do with Phoenix?"

A humble apology. I am to blame if I am failing my duty as a writer. I intend to explain how *profound* and how *long ago* were the shifts in the software industry *away* from the sort of project managements methods employed by Canada's government. When we return to our chronology, I want you armed with knowledge of the best practices and techniques known to the world in 2015.

My challenge is to condense three decades of evolutionary change across the industry into a cohesive chapter of this little book; and to do it without stretching your patience too far.

On my honour, I hope I can rise to that challenge.

Scrum

"A Major Management Discovery", according to Forbes Magazine[45].

Fellow historian, Gunther Verheyen, writes[46]:

> "At the OOPSLA[47] event of 1995, Ken Schwaber discussed Scrum in a 'Business Object Design and Implementation' workshop with Jeff Sutherland as a panel member for that event track."

Schwaber and Sutherland would later explain their conference presentation "essentially documented the learning [they] gained over the previous few years"[48].

Scrum was/is an idea based on key assertions about team development and product quality:

- The end state of a product cannot be known in advance.

---

[45] Steve Denning, "Scrum: A Major Management Discovery," Forbes, July 6, 2012, https://www.forbes.com/sites/stevedenning/2012/07/06/scrum-a-major-management-discovery/, https://archive.is/IMU1h.

[46] Verheyen, Gunther. "Scrum: A Brief History of a Long-Lived Hype." December 2020. Accessed March 3, 2023. https://guntherverheyen.com/wp-content/uploads/2020/12/Scrum-A-Brief-History-of-a-Long-Lived-Hype-Paper.pdf, https://archive.is/urehp.

[47] Object-Oriented Programming, Systems, Languages & Applications

[48] Scrum.org. "Scrum Guide." Accessed March 5, 2023. https://scrumguides.org/scrum-guide.html.

- Change is to be welcomed (even late in development).
- Requirements are an ever-evolving list of options.
- Product architecture is optimized to enable inexpensive change.
- Self-organizing teams produce the best architectures and designs.
- And frequent delivery of small batches of high-quality features is the best risk-mitigation strategy.

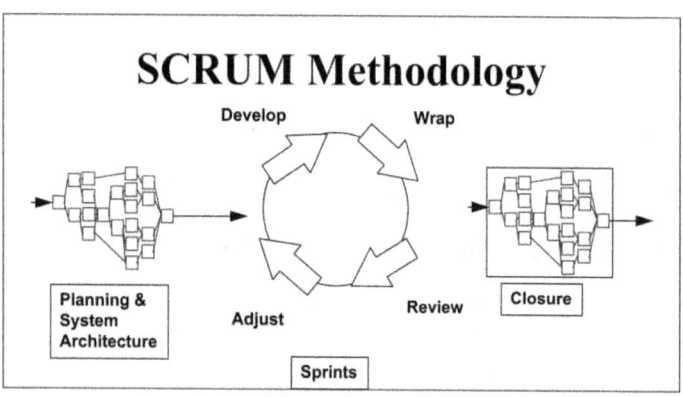

Exhibit 1: "SCRUM Methodology" (1995)

Figure 7: Diagram of Scrum, circa 1995, credit to Gunther Verheyen.

It helps to think of Scrum as a set of agreements that a team can adopt. They agree to work incrementally toward long-term goals in team units that are small and cross-functional. Rather than plan and build and launch a product over a long period, a Scrum team plans and builds and releases usable *increments* of that product in brief cycles (called "Sprints") — each release cycle is a month or less. The product grows with each increment.

In that regard, Scrum encouraged a development pattern similar to *MIL-STD-498*, and *The New New Product Development Game*: iterative and incremental development.

***

By 2015 (when we return to our chronology), Scrum was ubiquitous in tech startups and forward-looking IT enterprises everywhere. It was reaching peak "hype". It was simultaneously the new darling of publications like the Harvard Business Review[49] and the subject of hipster *ire* in millennial pop culture — for example, *Silicon Valley* (the sitcom) joked about Scrum in an episode in 2014.

---

[49] Barton, Dominic, and Mathias Herzog. "Embracing Agile." Harvard Business Review, 25 May 2016, https://hbr.org/2016/05/embracing-agile, https://archive.is/Ldopw.

Unfortunately for the Canadian taxpayers, Scrum had not yet disrupted the antiquated project management habits of the federal government.

Extreme Programming

Not only were *management* practices evolving, but software engineering *technique* had undergone thorough transformation many times over.

Long gone were the days of punch cards and reel-to-reel tapes. Programmers from Royce's or Brooks' era, had they time-travelled from the 1960's to the 90's, may have thought an advanced civilization of aliens had gifted their other-worldly technology.

I know that sounds like exaggeration, but I am quite serious. For example, we know from his notes that Leonardo da Vinci sketched wheeled vehicles that resembled a cart or carriage; but imagine Da Vinci had time-travelled to 1885 to meet Karl Benz — and there in Benz's workshop he would see the first gasoline-powered car.

Da Vinci could imagine the possibility of the automobile — a seat, axles, wheels. But the technological advancements required in metalwork, engine mechanics, petrochemical processing, these technologies would have seemed other-worldly.

Yes, I assert the technological distance between Da Vinci's sketches (*circa* 1500) and Benz's automobile in 1885 (385 years later) approximates the technological distance between, say, IBM's OS/360 of 1964 and the average pocket-sized flip-phones 30 years later.

Likewise, at the level of source code, the technological distance between COBOL (1960) and Python (1991) is as vast. It should surprise nobody that modern engineering practices became known as *Extreme Programming* (XP).[50]

Kent Beck, in *Extreme Programming Explained: Embrace Change*, asserted that high quality software is best produced by self-organizing teams with a high degree of autonomy and in increments in which analysis and development activities overlap. He illustrated the risks of segregating those activities by time and/or by personnel, and recommended pragmatic alternatives such as pair-programming, just-

---

[50] Kent Beck, Extreme Programming Explained: Embrace Change, 1st ed. (Reading, MA: Addison-Wesley Professional, 1999).

in-time requirements gathering, test-driven development, and continuous integration.

The many practices of XP have since been adopted by teams worldwide:

- Collective Code Ownership
- Continuous Integration (CI/CD)
- Customer Tests (BDD)
- Definition of Done
- Incremental Requirements
- Pair Programming
- Real Customer Involvement (UX Testing)
- Refactoring
- Spike Solutions
- Test-Driven Development (TDD)
- Unit Testing
- Version Control

Some on that list are so ubiquitous that young developers incorporate them without having learned of Extreme Programming. For example, some of my readers will associate many practices on that list with *DevOps* or other such trends.

Overall, XP offered a practical and actionable approach to software development that mitigates risk and optimizes for flexible architecture, maintainable code, and ever-evolving requirements.

***

Given these advancements in development technique, are you growing more curious why Canada's government, in 2015, would manage digital product development as though it is still 1965?

Agilemanifesto.org

Then, in 2001, a modest website was published that would not only help dispel the Waterfall myth but would help forge a new mythology more appropriate for a new era.

The authors of the website included known advocates of lightweight iterative and incremental development practices. For example, the group included the pioneers of XP, the co-authors of Scrum, and the inventors of Wiki. They all shared a mutual goal to uncover better ways of developing software by doing it and helping others to do it.[51]

The website's singular purpose is the publication of the so-named *Manifesto for Agile Software Development*[52]. This is the document that coined the term "Agile" for use in project management and software product development. Overall, the Agile Manifesto has had a significant impact on the way organizations approach project management, business strategy, and technology development.

We will see more on this topic in future chapters.

The Waterfall is Dead

How do myths die?

Myths tend to expand over time. They take on new elements or themes — but they always remain rooted in their original cultural context. The Waterfall, for example, is rooted in the assertion that software must

[51] Kent Beck, Mike Beedle, Arie van Bennekum, Alistair Cockburn, Ward Cunningham, Martin Fowler, James Grenning, Jim Highsmith, Andrew Hunt, Ron Jeffries, Jon Kern, Brian Marick, Robert C. Martin, Steve Mellor, Ken Schwaber, Jeff Sutherland, Dave Thomas
[52] The Manifesto for Agile Software Development, accessed March 5, 2023, http://agilemanifesto.org/

be produced by a pre-conceived *sequence* of activities — and the cultural context was mid-20th century when the cost of changing a software program was extremely high.

But the cultural context changed profoundly. In the 21st century, the cost of changing a well-designed software program *can* be trivial. And, for a growing number of people, the key elements of Waterfall no longer match their direct experience — it is outdated and problematic. When asking the question, "How do we produce software?", we increasingly find success in iterative and incremental patterns.

When we return to our chronology in 2015, the new mythology, "Agile", and the ideas in which it is rooted had evolved for at least 30+ years.

Project Management Institute

Following the publication of AgileManifesto.org, and having noticed the worldwide attention it earned, the Project Management Institute (PMI) began to adapt.

PMI has *not* been a market *leader* with respect to software engineering or digital systems management.

Personally, I respect they are a purveyor of techniques for critical path planning and conventional (not digital) projects. That is their wheelhouse, so-to-speak, and their certifications/training have expanded Waterfall mythology for many years. With respect to more modern/idiomatic software development practices, on the other hand, they have been a market *follower*.

But I give credit where it's due.

In 2013, PMI quietly published an extension to their widely known PMBOK (Project Management Body of Knowledge). The book was aptly called *Software Extension to PMBOK® Guide – Fifth Edition (2013)*[53].

Page after page, the book describes iterative and incremental development methods and recommends their application in the realm of software development. The existence of the book is a signal that even PMI recognized the need to abandon the Waterfall myth.

Unfortunately, few project managers are aware of the book.

---

[53] Project Management Institute. (2013). PMI PMBOK® Guide and Software Extension to PMBOK® Guide 5th edition [Web page]. Retrieved from https://www.pmi.org/pmbok-guide-standards/foundational/pmbok/software-extension-5th-edition, https://archive.is/l4qna.

Chaos Report 2015

The publication of the Agile Manifesto and the worldwide attention it achieved provided a rare and crucially important opportunity.

For the first time in three quarters of a century, since the invention of the computer (the Turing machine), it became possible to empirically study the relative efficacy of two dominant and ubiquitous digital project management paradigms: *Waterfall versus Agile*.

The *Chaos Report* is published by The Standish Group. I will share details from the report published in 2015. That document is helpful to our little book for at least three reasons:

- By 2015, the Chaos database included a statistically significant sample size of both so-called *Waterfall* and so-called *Agile* projects.
- A summary of the report was freely available online,[54]
- ...and, therefore freely available to the consultants, bureaucrats, and parliamentarians

---

[54] The Standish Group, "CHAOS Report 2015," The Standish Group International, Inc., 2015, https://standishgroup.com/sample_research_files/CHAOSReport2015-Final.pdf, https://archive.is/ne3cH.

managing the development of the Phoenix payroll system.

Proponents of the Waterfall approach had long argued that sequential gating provided better control of scope and risk. They argued that Agile methods were mere fad — juvenile and suitable only for small projects. They argued incremental development was a dangerously unserious way create large infrastructure. They were adamant that careful planning and analysis *must* be done up front and by specialists.

On the other hand, proponents of Agile practices (e.g., Scrum, XP, Kanban — the derivations were multiplying by this time) argued that iterative and incremental patterns allow rapid course-corrections and therefore reduce risk. They scoff at the Waterfall as an archaic idea, outdated and obsolete.

Who is right?

Is one paradigm superior to the other?

Which paradigm is best suited for large projects?

Which paradigm is the better risk-mitigation strategy?

The results published in the Chaos Report were very clear, overwhelmingly one-sided, and surprising to many. One of the tables is so striking and unambiguous, the debate is quite *over*.

The table showed that, across all 10,000 projects represented in the data, Agile methods succeeded more than 3 times as often as Waterfall.

SIZE	METHOD	SUCCESSFUL	CHALLENGED	FAILED
All Size Projects	Agile	39%	52%	9%
	Waterfall	11%	60%	29%
Large Size Projects	Agile	18%	59%	23%
	Waterfall	3%	55%	42%
Medium Size Projects	Agile	27%	62%	11%
	Waterfall	7%	68%	25%
Small Size Projects	Agile	58%	38%	4%
	Waterfall	44%	45%	11%

Figure 8: CHAOS RESOLUTION BY AGILE VERSUS WATERFALL. The resolution of all software projects from FY2011–2015 within the CHAOS database, segmented by the agile process and Waterfall method. The total number of software projects is over 10,000.

Shocking differences, however, were found as the data were categorized by project size:

· In the largest projects, the Waterfall approach was successful only 3% of the time. While an Agile approach was successful 18% of the time — 6x better.

- Large Waterfall projects fail at a rate of 42%, with Agile projects failing at ½ that rate.

Authors of the report note "in many cases, larger projects *never* return value to an organization." And "government projects had the highest failure rate at 24%."

It can be argued these numbers leave a lot to be desired. Despite Agile methods showing *six times* the success rate of Waterfall in the largest projects, there is much room for improvement.

So, please return to the table and notice the success rates of *small* projects. Small, Agile projects show a success rate of 58% and failure only 4%.

The authors propose "to create a winning hand, the trump cards are the [1] Agile process and [2] small projects." They assert, "only in very rare cases do projects need to be larger and longer. Most, if not all, large, complex, multi-year projects are unnecessary."

To mitigate risk, the data show we ought to "break up large software projects into multiple small projects, with early delivery for success, quicker return on value, and greater customer and user satisfaction".

***

The Chaos Report is published periodically, the most recent was 2020. Their findings remain consistent.

Furthermore, their results have since been corroborated by Digital.ai, Boston Consulting Group, McKinsey, Info-Tech, and others.

All of This Was Known in 2015

In 2015, the Waterfall myth was a half-century old and thoroughly discredited. Superior techniques were also mainstream and at least 30 years old.

As we continue our chronological review in the next chapter, I believe you will notice these phenomena:

- The Phoenix myth invoked confidence in the new digital *tools*.
- The Waterfall myth helped cultivate confidence in the *process*.

But confidence in either the tools or the process was, in early 2015, entirely unwarranted, irrational, and tragically expensive.

The Trudeau Era, 1st Term

Justin Trudeau, Canada's 23rd Prime Minister, took office in 2015.

***

Adele said *Hello*. Rachel Platten taught us her *Fight Song*. And Paul McCartney recorded with Kanye West and Rihanna (nobody saw *that* coming). Meanwhile, The Tragically Hip was on tour and can you guess who was singing with Van Halen?

***

When Members of Parliament returned after the election, the atmosphere was different. The winds of change had swept through the offices in Ottawa. "Sunny ways", waxed Trudeau.

But the sun didn't shine for long. It is said, *no project plan survives contact with reality*: bureaucrats and parliamentarians would soon learn that lesson the hard way. It was in *this* term that the Phoenix would ignite and explode.

The mythical Phoenix is immortal and lives several hundred years before burning and being reborn from its own ashes. Some stories tell us there is no known method to kill the Phoenix. It is a creature of great power and resilience.

However, other stories suggest it has a weakness. Some legends say the Phoenix can be killed by a silver arrow or by being drowned or suffocated.

As it happens, the Phoenix is no match for bureaucracy.

2015, October 9

One of the first documents presented to the new parliamentarians was a detailed timeline of the Phoenix launch plan.[55]

The *intended* sequence of events was meticulously documented. January 29th, for example, was labelled "Go-live Recommendation".

[55] "A-2016-00660: Final Versions of Transition to Phoenix Documents - PSPC," Scribd, accessed March 15, 2022, https://www.scribd.com/document/351277799/A-2016-00660-Final-Versions-of-Transition-to-Phoenix-Documents-PSPC.

(Spoiler alert: they recommended "go".)

We will see, as I share the evidence with you, they followed the schedule against all odds.

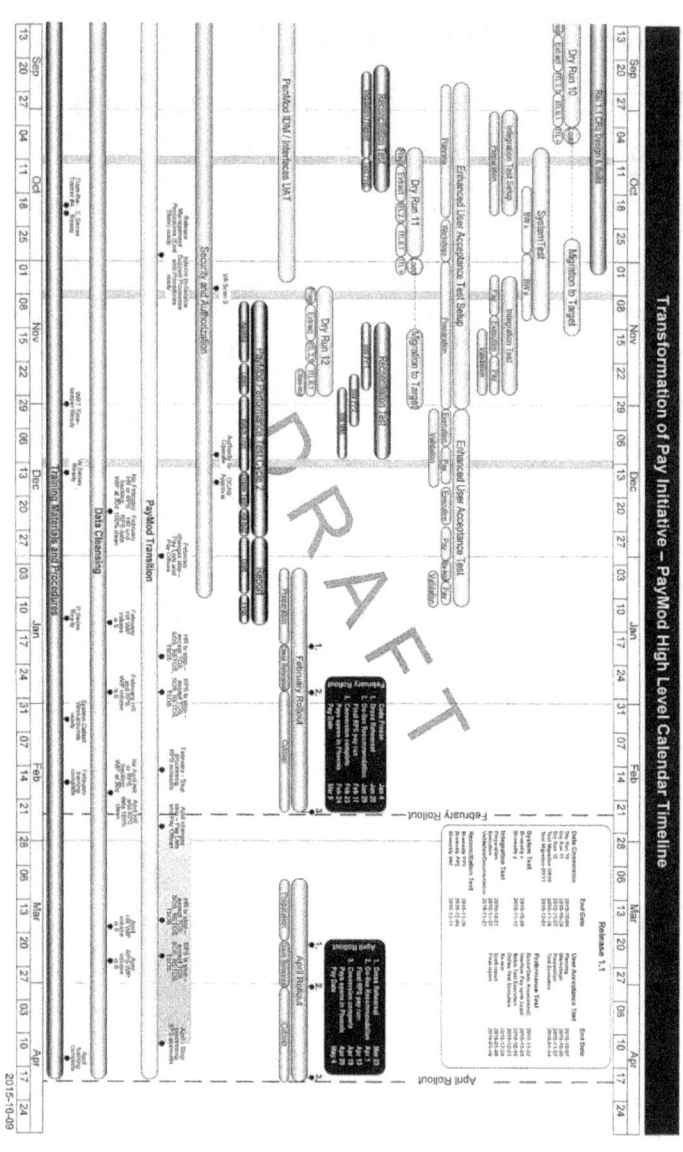

Figure 9: PayMod High Level Calendar Timeline

2015, December 14

A "status update" was presented to the Senior Project Advisory Committee (SPAC) by Kristine Renic, Director General of the Phoenix project (a.k.a., TPA: Transformation of Pay Administration Initiative).

The presentation deserves careful study by project managers and, especially, by *psychologists*. How such terrible news could be presented with such optimism is wondrous and awesome — and frightening. (See the slides for yourself. [56])

There are two crucial features of this report.

First, the bulk of the presentation is designed to *glorify the plan*. We can imagine their excitement — bureaucrats who poured years of their career into this project were now talking with a new set of parliamentarians. They wanted to make a good impression, put everyone's mind at ease. "The project is on track to deliver the expected outcomes", they said.

---

[56] Government of Canada. "Final Versions of Transition to Phoenix Documents." [PDF file]. https://www.scribd.com/document/351277850/A-2016-00669-Final-Versions-of-Transition-to-Phoenix-Documents-TBS. (Accessed March 3, 2023).)

The project was "on scope and on budget", they explained. *Nothing to worry about.*

Second, buried near the end of the slide presentation is an "Issue & Risks Dashboard". The topmost outstanding risk states:

> "Phoenix system may not be stable upon code freeze and through dress rehearsal prior to the system moving into production."

Everyone involved agreed this was *highly probable* and would have *massive impact*. According to estimates, the likelihood of that outcome was in the 80th percentile.

***

Let's you and I play a game...If we were together in Las Vegas at a Roulette wheel and I told you there's an 80% probability the next ball will land on black, how much would you bet on red?

A few billion?

2015, December 21

Ten federal departments, such as Royal Canadian
Mounted Police (RCMP) and Canada Revenue Agency
(CRA), responded to a "Readiness assessment of
Phoenix". Feedback from those departments was
collected, in part, during a conference call on December
21[57].

Nothing about their feedback should have inspired
confidence in the readiness of Phoenix. They expressed
serious concern. HR personnel, for example, had yet to
see even *see* the system.

Notes from the meeting highlight two critical problems:

- "Heads of HR feel insufficiently informed and
  confident".
- "Departments lack evidence to support
  readiness."

---

[57] Public Services and Procurement Canada, "December 21, 2015, Dept.
Review - Phoenix," embedded in "December 21, 2015, Dept. Review -
Phoenix," accessed on March 5, 2023,
https://www.scribd.com/document/344170694/December-21-2015-
Dept-Review-Phoenix.

For those of you who do not speak the language of officialdom, that is how bureaucrats signal a five-alarm fire.

2016, January 13

Further feedback from those federal departments was filed with the Treasury Board. Their submissions are alarming:

- "No end to end testing."
- "Less than 50% success rate."
- "Testing results unknown."
- "Training at the last minute."
- "System readiness is questionable."
- "Outstanding defects are still critical and not fixed."
- "Unknown if collective agreements are well coded into Pheonix (sic)."
- "The error rate is going up."
- "Pheonix (sic) only calculated with 2 digits where the collective bargaining agreements requires 3 digits."
- "Privacy issue not resolved where members of the cluster can access other department's data."

2016, January 18

Not all myths are based on fantasy and fiction. For example: government, currency, law — these are myths that rely on shared understanding and social agreements.

Currency, for example, has real-world consequences and effects — it has value because people agree that it has value. Money is a contract (an IOU) that transmits value through time. Our confidence in the myth grows each time a person accepts money in exchange for a good or service, and each time a person deposits money into a bank and returns later in their life to withdraw it.

But what of mythical management strategies? How does confidence grow, for example, in myths like employment, teamwork, contracts, projects? And, for the myths relevant to our little book: Agile? Waterfall? Why do people *believe* in such things?

(We will discuss the Agile myth further in later chapters.)

The Waterfall myth is fantastical, superstitious — it is based entirely on wishful thinking and is upheld by faith.

The Waterfall

— a poem by David Sabine & ChatGPT

*Thus, it was spoken, from this day forth, The
following sequence shall be of utmost worth,
Optimal results shall it bring forth, To be adhered
to by all, from South to North.*

*Let us follow this righteous way, And in our deeds,
let us not go astray, For through obedience, we
shall be blessed, And in abundance, we shall surely
be caressed.*

Because *business* results and the quality of a digital
system cannot be measured until the Waterfall runs its
course and a "launch" event occurs, how are
bureaucrats to know their project is on track?

On one hand, they could study the Phoenix system and
its operation — does the system function as it is
supposed to? By mid-January, evidence from test
results and the feedback from department heads
indicated very bad news in this regard. Perhaps
Phoenix had transformed into Medusa — the
bureaucrats were reluctant to look directly at it.

On the other hand, they could study the project *plan*
and their adherence to it. The answer to a difficult

question, "Will the new system be successful?", can be answered by an easier question: "How dutifully have we followed the plan?"[58] Like any faith-based mythology, the practitioners of Waterfall are often measured by their piety — their devotion and adherence to the tenets and practices of the faith.

So, right on schedule, the project leaders hired fellow faith leaders (project management consultants) to:

- Study the project plan.
- Confirm that the plan complied fully with the Treasury Board's requirements.
- And confirm the bureaucrats followed the plan dutifully.

S.I. Systems submitted a report[59] on January 18 to that effect.

It is crucially important to understand the consultants did not inspect the Phoenix system. They inspected only the documentation about the project. Their work, by design, was to talk with the directors of the project and ask them if they did a good job.

---

[58] Tip: Keyword search "Substitution Bias"
[59] "Report on the Phoenix Pay System by S.i. Systems" (2016), in Scribd [digital platform], accessed on March 10, 2023, https://www.scribd.com/document/344170107/S-I-Systems-Report.

The consultants met and interviewed 14 people:

- · Nine directors from PSPC,
- · One manager from the Phoenix Project Management office,
- · And Four directors/managers from IBM.

S.I. Systems submitted a persuasive slide deck showing that all the i's were dotted and all the t's were crossed. Through this remarkable exercise of CYA[60], the report declared that the project plan was flawless and the project leaders' work was exemplary. Their pious devotion to the Waterfall was beyond reproach.

Worthy of sizeable bonuses!

2016, January 20

Meanwhile, a *Summary of Phoenix Testing Results* was submitted. It included tests performed up to January 14.[61]

First, I will note there is little evidence of automated testing. For example, we might expect to see a coverage

---

[60] See also "Cover Your Ass".

[61] "January 20, 2016 Test Results - PSPC Phoenix," Scribd, accessed March 15, 2023, https://www.scribd.com/document/344170805/January-20-2016-Test-Results-PSPC-Phoenix.

report or sample test code. We might expect to see data showing test performance (how many milliseconds each test requires). We might expect to see code standards such as whether all tests are executed nightly, on every deployment, or every time new code is committed to the version-control system, *etc.*

Instead, the report spoke of integration testing in the past tense: "integration testing *was* to test...*etc*". And the report spoke of test cycles: "Pension testing *was* carried out in 47 test cycles."

Second, the report showed the system was not ready. Not even close.

By early 2016 there were 105 active collective agreements[62] and 80,000+ regulations. According to the test results, only 15,727 scenarios were executed with respect to "Phoenix Core Testing". Those tests show a failure rate up to 18% in key categories.

The report also explained that four cycles of bi-weekly pay were conducted with 86,000 accounts with a

[62] Office of the Auditor General of Canada. (2017). Report 1—The Phoenix Pay System. https://www.oag-bvg.gc.ca/internet/English/parl_oag_201711_01_e_42666.html, https://archive.is/oQRV6.

whopping 7.4% failure rate. (With 300,000 employees, that would be 577,200 errors per year.)

There were 124 known defects included in the report — 58 considered "major".

***

Let's you and I play another game...You ask to borrow my boat and I tell you there's 124 known defects that may cause it to sink in the middle of the lake. Do you still want the keys?

2016, January 29

The Treasury Board Secretariat hired Gartner to conduct a *PayMod Readiness Assessment*.[63] Gartner's report is dated February 11 but a copy was allegedly sent on January 29 to Gavin Liddy, Associate Deputy Minister and successor to Renée Jolicoeur.

---

[63] Gartner, "Best Practices for Implementing an HRMS System," Scribd, accessed March 23, 2023, https://www.scribd.com/document/344165319/Gartner-Report-From-TBS.

With hindsight, parliamentarians *two years later* would describe the Gartner report as "pretty damning". MP Kelly McCauley said in a PACP committee meeting in November 2017, "You read Gartner and it's like there's no way we should have gone forward."[64]

Some journalists described Gartner's report as deeply critical. In the Ottawa Citizen, James Bagnall wrote of the report:

> "...it was much less sanguine than that of S.I. Systems..."[65]

And as if to find Gavin Liddy uniquely culpable, Bagnall added:

> "Liddy would later testify before a House of Commons committee that he did not show the Gartner report to his boss Judy Foote until the summer."

---

[64] "Meeting No. 81 of the Standing Committee on Public Accounts (PACP)," 42nd Parliament, 1st Session (26 September 2017), https://www.ourcommons.ca/DocumentViewer/en/42-1/PACP/meeting-81/evidence, https://archive.is/1s8yG.

[65] Bagnall, J. (2018, June 22). Risks unheeded, journey without end: The seeds of the tortured Phoenix pay project were planted three decades ago. Ottawa Citizen. Retrieved March 2, 2023, from https://ottawacitizen.com/news/politics/risks-unheeded-journey-without-end-the-seeds-of-the-tortured-phoenix-pay-project-were-planted-three-decades-ago, https://archive.is/vK758.

I appreciate Mr. Bagnall's perspective (and have read his reportage extensively while conducting research for this book) but I find Liddy no more culpable than anyone else.

Did he sit on information rather than share it with the Public Services Minister? *Yes.* Did a hundred others also sit on the same information? *Yes.* Had the information been provided to parliamentarians earlier; would it have caused them to intervene? *Certainly not.*

Read it if you wish, but their 61-page report included the evidence we have already seen in the pages of this book. And in typical fashion, the consultants were non-committal and vague in their recommendations. For example, one of the "key conclusions" they label "critical":

- "Gartner has identified only one criterion with a high probability of occurring, and a high negative impact and that is with Testing and the implications of outstanding defects, and yet to be identified defects."

Oh? Only *one* problem? Just the *one* "criterion" that it is highly probable the system doesn't work and is a steaming pile of defects?

And another example:

- "Gartner believes Support requests have a high probability of rising post go-live, _but_ the ability of Departmental HR staff and the Pay Centre to deal with these is unknown — there is insufficient information to determine this. The potential adverse impact of the inability to provide support is _moderate_."

_Oh?_ Is that all? Just the "high probability" that HR staff will be absolutely swamped with support requests? But ("but"!?) we are only _moderately_ confident that they can't handle it.

(The mental gymnastics in those statements is astounding.)

If McCauley or Bagnall or others are looking for evidence that _they should-a known better_, Gartner's report is not it. Gartner's consultants appear, to me, to be as entranced by the Waterfall and Phoenix myths as everyone else.

I understand I may stand alone with this argument, but it is my professional opinion Gartner's report helped persuade bureaucrats and parliamentarians that launching Phoenix was *imperative*. Phoenix was *too big to fail*. Two points in the report stand out:

First, Gartner warned that delaying the launch would cause a psychological collapse in "momentum" and "reputation" of the Phoenix:

> "delay will reduce project momentum...[and] have a severe reputational impact on the project...this will drive scrutiny and complicate the next go-live date." (p.35)

Second, Gartner notes there are other, massive projects underway that intersect with Phoenix. Delaying the launch of Phoenix, they argue, would cause a domino effect with expensive consequences: "financial impacts will accrue...re-work...re-start...staffing adjustment, *etc.*"

Gartner's report changed nothing. In fact, I believe Gartner's report further fueled the prevailing myths.

Flame is *necessary* to enable renewal; and turbulent Whitewater rapids *always* give way to a tranquil river.

"Go/No-Go"

In a bureaucracy like Canada's federal government, the "Go/No-Go" date of a large project is supremely ceremonial.

January 29 of 2016 was a Friday. It was the last workday of the month and was identified on the project plan, quite arbitrarily, as the "Go-Live Recommendation" date.

For parliamentarians and high-level stakeholders, Waterfall projects can be a disorienting experience. Through the *years* of "strategic planning", Phoenix stakeholders would have felt engaged, influential, and important. But when the budget was approved, a "project management office" took over and, as though a boomerang was thrown, there was nothing left to do but wait.

A few years of "requirements gathering" followed, and "design", then two years of "implementation" and "testing".

"Go/No-Go" events function like a signal that the boomerang is returning. The signal is: Wake up everyone! Answer the call! Your wise plan has materialized. Bask in its glow. You, once again, have an important decision to make: Will you release the Phoenix?

In reality, it was just another Friday and nobody intended to abort or delay the plans to unplug the old payroll systems. The ceremony had in fact been renamed from "Go/No-Go" (which is a convention) to "Go-Live Recommendation" — leaving no doubt of their intentions.

To force the use of the not-ready, known-to-be-defective Phoenix program was *the plan* — and as we have observed in the mountain of evidence, *the plan* was sacrosanct.

***

My dear reader, had the "Go/No-Go" date been *more* than mere ceremony, had they taken a sincere look at the facts, everything that followed could have been prevented. Everyone involved saw the evidence before them — the same evidence you and I have studied together. They could have used the information, but they did not.

Two years later, in a report by the Auditor General of Canada, they would write:

> "Before going ahead with implementing Phoenix, Phoenix executives knew about serious problems with it, including high security risks and privacy risks. They also knew that the new pay system could not perform critical functions, such as processing requests for retroactive pay or automatically calculating certain types of pay. They also had a summary of test results highlighting major defects found through testing that were still not resolved."[66]

And in a report produced by the Senate in summer of 2018, they would write:

> "Phoenix did not fail due to unforeseen events or challenging circumstances. Nor did it fail due to a single error or mistake. Rather, it failed due to a series of avoidable, poor management decisions."[67]

---

[66] Office of the Auditor General of Canada. (2018). Building and implementing the Phoenix pay system [Report]. Office of the Auditor General of Canada. Retrieved from https://www.oag-bvg.gc.ca/internet/English/parl_oag_201805_01_e_43033.html, https://archive.is/pkUEz.

[67] Senate of Canada. (2018). Phoenix pay system: Lessons learned. Retrieved from https://sencanada.ca/content/sen/committee/421/NFFN/reports/NFFN_Phoenix_Report_32_WEB_e.pdf, https://archive.is/sA7Wy.

(In case you are curious, the answer is: no. Not one. Not even one of the managers was fired.)

A quality assurance engineer could have sounded the alarm. A senior developer could have blown the whistle. A project manager could have raised a red flag. An HR executive could have rung the bell. The Deputy Minister to Judy Foote, George Da Pont, could have screamed bloody murder. Or Judy Foote herself, the Public Services Minister, could have hit the panic button. It is even conceivable, had the information bubbled up to the Prime Minister's office, even Justin Trudeau could have pulled the plug.

But, despite all the evidence before them, would you believe the decision to go ahead was *unanimous?*

Not a single voice of dissent. In a meeting of the Standing Committee on Public Accounts (PACP) in September 2017[68], MP Gérard Deltell would press for details:

Deltell:

---

[68] "Meeting No. 81 of the Standing Committee on Public Accounts (PACP)," 42nd Parliament, 1st Session (26 September 2017), https://www.ourcommons.ca/DocumentViewer/en/42-1/PACP/meeting-81/evidence, https://archive.is/1s8yG.

"How many deputy ministers said go and how many said no go?"

Yaprak Baltacioglu, Secretary of the Treasury:

"There were no no-gos."

***

Some say they didn't have a choice.

I say there's always a choice.

They made the wrong one.

2016, February 18
The Point of No Return

A report was submitted by Brigitte Fortin, Assistant Deputy Minister at PSPC, and Rosanna Di Paola, Associate Assistant Deputy Minister at PWGSC. The report represents their official recommendation to the Minister, Judy Foote, to proceed as planned.

In an OGGO committee meeting the following summer, MP Judy Foote said, "as the minister responsible, I was told we were in a ready-to-go state, that Phoenix was ready to go."[69]

In an OGGO committee meeting a year later, MP Nick Whalen summarized the content of that report:[70]

"Where are we on Technology?
...Ready to Go!

Where are we on Process?
...Ready to Go!

Where are we on People?
...Ready to Go!"

2016, February 24

For the people closest the actual work (I am referring to the software engineers and compensation advisors expected to deploy and use the new systems), the

---

[69] House of Commons. (n.d.). Standing Committee on Government Operations and Estimates Evidence - OGGO (42-1) - No. 025 - House of Commons of Canada. Retrieved March 5, 2023, from https://www.ourcommons.ca/DocumentViewer/en/42-1/OGGO/meeting-25/evidence#Int-9029986, https://archive.is/tFcRx.

[70] "Meeting 88 - Standing Committee on Government Operations and Estimates," House of Commons, 42nd Parliament, 1st Session (2017), https://www.ourcommons.ca/DocumentViewer/en/42-1/OGGO/meeting-88/evidence, https://archive.is/kWk1M.

instructions they were being given must have seemed 100% insane.

In previous weeks, compensation advisors had been warned to brace themselves with workarounds to an ever-growing list of defects. They were already overloaded with a backlog of errors related to the botched rollout of a new HR system. HR personnel were being laid off across the country. The Pay Centre in Miramichi was staffed with hundreds of new employees, and none had laid their own eyes on the mythical Phoenix.

Developers were being told to ignore hundreds of known defects. Software development managers were calling meetings and making pronouncements about "2-stage rollout" and "dressed rehearsals" and "cutovers" and "reconciliation tests".

February 24th was the day payroll staff were to begin using Phoenix to prepare the upcoming March 9th paycheques.

2016, March 9

Phoenix was used to prepare paycheques for 120,000 people. It is estimated that 40,000 of those employees were paid incorrect amounts.

2016, March 10

At a parliamentary committee meeting, the Minister of Public Services Judy Foote reported:

> "The new pay system, called Phoenix, was implemented just two weeks ago, on February 24, and the first pay cycle [March 9] has proven to be a success."[71]

A success?

And her Deputy Minister, George Da Pont, corroborated:

---

[71] "Meeting No. 6 - Standing Committee on Government Operations and Estimates (OGGO)", House of Commons Canada, accessed on March 15, 2023, https://www.ourcommons.ca/DocumentViewer/en/42-1/OGGO/meeting-6/evidence, https://archive.is/p0Cy0.

"I think people often say that in government you can't effectively manage big projects. I want to say that this was an enormous project...

I'm not going to declare victory yet, but we went through the first pay period this week, and it worked very well. I'd feel a little more comfortable going through at least one or two more pay periods before I crack the champagne open, but I do want to say that I think this has been a remarkable job by the team..."

2016, March 31

This date marks the end of the federal government's "performance pay cycle". Canadians would eventually learn through a formal inquiry by MP Steven MacKinnon that bonuses for the period paid to PSPC executives amounted to (collectively) $4,827,913 — an average of $14,200 per executive.[72]

---

[72] Treasury Board of Canada Secretariat, "Performance Pay," (Ottawa: Government of Canada, 2011). https://www.scribd.com/document/344172564/OPQ-841-Performance-Pay.

2016, April 1

The project plan indicates this date was the "Go/No-Go" decision for the 2nd stage of the rollout. As you and I have already discussed, it was purely ceremonial.

2016, April 13

The Regional Pay Systems (RPS) would process their last paycheques. Phoenix was the new system of record — this was called "cutover".

2016, April 19

Parliamentarians had become aware of severe payroll problems. There was an interesting exchange at the OGGO committee meeting between MP Steven Blaney and the Secretary of the Treasury, Yaprak Baltacioglu:[73]

Blaney:

---

[73] Parliament of Canada. House of Commons. Standing Committee on Government Operations and Estimates. Evidence - OGGO (42-1) - No. 8 - Meeting No. 8. 30 November 2016. https://www.ourcommons.ca/DocumentViewer/en/42-1/OGGO/meeting-8/evidence, https://archive.is/JcGZU.

"You are now preparing to implement the second phase of the Phoenix pay system.

We have learned that public servants are not receiving their pay, specifically Canadian Coast Guard employees, who return from several weeks or months on assignments abroad for Canada only to discover in horror that their pay has not been deposited.

...can you reassure us that for those who have been negatively impacted, the situation has been corrected?"

Baltacioglu:

"Yes, sir.

...Before the next phase of departments are brought onboard to the new system, Public Services and Procurement Canada, which is the responsible department, is checking with every department and identifying the areas that we have problems with...If they feel we're not ready, they will delay. If they feel that 99% of it is going to work, then we will go forward."

That response would come back to haunt Baltacioglu in November 2018 at a PACP committee meeting. In a tense exchange, she was pressed to explain *who* advised the Minister of Public Services to proceed with the 2nd stage rollout and *how* was the decision made despite there already being hundreds of thousands of payroll errors from the 1st stage:[74]

MP Gérard Deltell:

"10 days before pulling the trigger on the second phase of implementation, a House of Commons committee held a meeting. That was on April 19, 2016. Ms. Baltacioglu, secretary of the Treasury Board, was in attendance. This is what she said at the meeting: '…If they feel we're not ready, they will delay. If they feel that 99% of it is going to work, then we will go forward.'

Madam, has there been 99% success?"

Baltacioglu:

"Clearly not, sir."

Deltell:

[74] Parliament of Canada. House of Commons. Standing Committee on Public Accounts. Evidence. 42nd Parliament, 1st Session, Meeting 81. Accessed March 5, 2023. https://www.ourcommons.ca/DocumentViewer/en/42-1/PACP/meeting-81/evidence, https://archive.is/1s8yG.

"We are to understand, then, that when you made the decision, 99% of the people involved were telling you that it was going to work. Is that correct?"

Baltacioglu:

"Sir, what I said was that they, meaning PSPC, would move forward only if they were 99% sure."

Deltell:

"They were 99% sure?"

Baltacioglu:

"The 99% was used as an assurance that...was understood. At the time, the managers of this program felt that they had workarounds for some of the risks, and they had management strategies for the risks."

Deltell:

"Madam, you're the one who set the bar at 99%. Was it 99% when you pushed the button for the second time?"

Baltacioglu:

"I didn't push the button...We are a central agency...We made sure that everybody was aware and that PSPC was aware that this was a no-fail project, and they felt that they were ready."

Deltell:

"If you're not the one who pushed the button, who did it?"

Baltacioglu:

"The authority given by the government was to the Minister of Public Services and Procurement Canada..."

Deltell:

"You're talking about a group, and I'm talking about someone. Who's the one who called the shot?"

Baltacioglu:

"The decision...rests with Public Services and Procurement Canada."

Deltell:

"You didn't answer my question, Madam. Who is the one who said to the minister, 'Push the button. Go.'"

Baltacioglu:

"The Minister of Public Services and Procurement. The deputy minister at the time would have been the one to give the advice."

Deltell:

"Who's that?"

Baltacioglu:

"It was Mr. George Da Pont."

2016, April 30

George Da Pont took early retirement.[75]

2016, May 4

The first pay day of stage 2.

Phoenix was used to prepare paycheques for nearly 300,000 employees across 101 federal departments.

75 Kathryn May, Ottawa Citizen, "Two more deputy ministers retire," March 9, 2023, accessed March 10, 2023, https://ottawacitizen.com/news/national/two-more-deputy-ministers-retire/, https://archive.is/e7poF.

2016, June[76]

The Public Service Alliance of Canada (a union representing federal employees) filed a formal compliant with the Public Service Labour Relations Employment Board.[77] They would argue that, by failing to provide timely and accurate pay, the employer broke the law.

2016, July 11

Canadians had learned of the mess. Journalists were collecting and publishing stories that would help Canadians and parliamentarians understand the extent of the tragedy unfolding.

- "I had a contract...that ended in January...I am still being paid."[78]
- "Please stop paying me...I retired three years ago."

---

[76] I have been unable to confirm the exact date.

[77] CBC News. (2016, September 1). Phoenix payroll hearings should address labour complaint, says union. CBC News. https://www.cbc.ca/news/canada/ottawa/phoenix-payroll-hearings-labour-complaint-1.3760795, https://archive.is/zz7dW.

[78] CBC News, "Public servants, too much pay," last modified June 28, 2016, https://www.cbc.ca/news/canada/ottawa/public-servants-too-much-pay-1.3670415, https://archive.is/SLXKg.

- "I was working for Health Canada and deployed back to DND. I am currently getting 2 paycheques, one from each department."

2016, July 19

News broke of a data breach.[79]

It was reported that managers using Phoenix had access to details about employees who did not work for them — including Social Insurance Numbers and other confidential information.

You, my dear reader, might remember this concern was raised in January by HR department heads. Remember this?

- "Privacy issue not resolved where members of the cluster can access other department's data."

---

[79] CBC News. "Privacy Commissioner asked to investigate Phoenix pay system breach." CBC News, 5 July 2016, https://www.cbc.ca/news/politics/phoenix-privacy-breach-wier-cavoukian-1.3691866, https://archive.is/NAJul.

2016, July 22

Canada's Privacy Commissioner announced he would launch an investigation into the breach.[80]

(Note: It appears that it took Canada's government six months to transmit news of this breach from department heads to the Privacy Commissioner, and only after it was publicly reported by journalists.)

2016, July 28

Firefighting continued. People and money were being thrown at the problem.

Three key executives from PWGSC were questioned at an OGGO committee meeting:[81]

- Marie Lemay, Deputy Minister
- Gavin Liddy, Associate Deputy Minister

---

[80] CBC News, "Phoenix privacy breach highlights risks of mandatory overtime: former privacy commissioner," CBC News, last modified July 10, 2016, accessed March 9, 2023, https://www.cbc.ca/news/politics/phoenix-privacy-breach-wiercavoukian-1.3691866, .

[81] House of Commons, Standing Committee on Government Operations and Estimates, Evidence, 42nd Parl, 1st Sess, 24th meeting (n.d.), online: https://www.ourcommons.ca/DocumentViewer/en/42-1/OGGO/meeting-24/evidence, https://archive.is/7b4GN.

- Rosanna Di Paola, Associate Assistant Deputy Minister

Parliamentarians heard, after laying off 1,000+ people across the country, managers were now begging people to return to their job. A "temporary pay unit" was established in Gatineau, Quebec, where 57 compensation advisors had been re-hired. At an estimated $20 million, the Gatineau facility would support 115 payroll staff "in the coming weeks". Another 50 were being hired in Winnipeg. 40 in Miramichi. Gavin Liddy did some helpful math, saying "that's about 240 people."

A far cry from George Da Pont's comments a few months earlier (e.g., "crack the champagne open"), Marie Lemay shared, "We're not saying this is a success, by a long shot."

She added:

> "We will learn a lot from this — a lot. We will put in place and make sure that people get paid, and we will make the system better and make it what it's supposed to be. The transition is much more difficult and much longer than we thought."

Everyone was trying to wrap their heads around the extent and cost of the problem. The project budget was around $300 million — I cannot fault them for thinking the system could be "fixed" for a *fraction* of that cost. MP Eric Wier asked the witnesses, "Can you provide any kind of overall estimate of the total cost of this Phoenix boondoggle?...Do you have any sense of the overall magnitude of what this is going to cost Canadian taxpayers?"

Lemay, in response:

"The measures we've taken right now are costing $15 to $20 million. We're in the process of looking at other things, so we'll soon be able to provide the additional costs."

Weir:

"If you could keep this committee up to date on those costs, I think we'd greatly appreciate it."

Lemay:

"I will, with pleasure."

But her optimism was not grounded. Consider her promise to report "the" additional costs — that word implies the final amount could be known and would be finite.

It is clear from that evidence that nobody had the faintest idea the scale nor nature of the chaos. The metaphor playing in their minds went something like this:

A car was manufactured; it won't start; let's replace the battery and get the car back on the road.

Even a year later, everyone from parliamentarians to journalists were talking of "fixing" Phoenix. Two years later they would talk of "stabilizing" Phoenix. The fact of the matter, Phoenix was not done. It was incomplete. And now it was an inferno.

And their mistake, I argue, is in thinking that the problem had any boundaries at all. A more appropriate metaphor might be:

A cruise ship was launched into the ocean, pre-loaded with thousands of passengers, before the hull was complete; and as it sinks, let's bail water and finish construction of the hull.

***

At the same meeting, MP Yasmin Ratansi asked about the morale of staff in Miramichi. Donna Lackie, a public sector union executive, shared:

> "I will tell you that the morale in Miramichi is at its absolute lowest. Last night I received an email from one of our members in Miramichi who is so depressed that in her email she told me they had found an employee in the bathroom crying the other day. I shared that email last night at 10 o'clock with the deputy minister and have asked that on-site mental health experts be brought in to support the workers in Miramichi — not a 24-hour EAP officer on a phone. We need on-site mental health to support these people. They're carrying the weight of the entire federal public service on their shoulders."

2016, September

At a labour board hearing, Rosanna Di Paola was under fire. She explained, if she could do it all over again, she "would have made the argument that training be mandatory for all users"[82]. That response didn't go over well as it appeared she was suggesting the only problem with Phoenix was human error due to lack of training.

When pressed on this point, she dug herself into a hole by deflecting accountability:

- "As long as people enter [information] wrong, it will be wrong."
- "We underestimated the time it took people to adapt to the new technology. The learning curve just seemed to be much longer than we expected."
- She explained some of the payroll errors were caused by employees who hadn't filled out their timecards properly.
- And (here's a doozy) "You may have heard 80,000 people are having pay problems. *Those are not Phoenix-related issues.*"

I believe Di Paola answered the questions put to her with utmost sincerity. That is unfortunate for at least two reasons:

---

[82] National Post, "Bureaucrats accused of blaming workers for Phoenix pay system errors as DND staff get training deadline," accessed March 4, 2023, https://nationalpost.com/news/politics/bureaucrats-accused-of-blaming-workers-for-phoenix-pay-system-errors-as-dnd-staff-get-training-deadline, https://archive.is/lbWbr.

First, because she did utter the words, "those are not Phoenix-related issues" — when one's foot goes that far into one's mouth, there is no way to recover. What everyone heard was (in other words) *there's nothing wrong with the computer system or the project — everything would be better if everyone had simply followed my plan and taken my advice to get trained.*

(Yet another example of faith-based mythology.)

Second, because nobody was in the mood for explanations or deflections. It is likely, even if she had taken a different tact, they were not in the mood for apologies or contrition either. They had their pitchforks; they were hunting witches; and this was Di Paola's last opportunity to avoid public defenestration.

2016, October

Days later, Di Paola was shuffled out of the line of fire into a new job.[83]

---

[83] May, Kathryn. "Bureaucrat who led Phoenix project shuffled aside in executive shakeup." Ottawa Citizen, 19 September 2016, https://ottawacitizen.com/news/national/bureaucrat-who-led-phoenix-project-shuffled-aside-in-executive-shakeup/, https://archive.is/RgTQV.

2016, November

PWGSC published an RFI (Request for Information) seeking help to finish and fix Phoenix.[84]

An RFI is a special type of financial instrument. It is not a request for quote or proposal (i.e., RFQ, RFP). It is an admission of uncertainty.

An RFI says: we need help, we know this is a giant problem and we have no idea what it might cost. Given the publicity around this issue, the enterprises who would respond to the RFI knew Canada's government was waving a blank cheque.

2016, December

As scheduled and approved earlier in the year, bonuses were paid to Phoenix executives.

---

[84] Government of Canada. (2016). Request for Information (RFI) In-Service Support for Government of Canada Pay System For Public Services and Procurement Canada (PSPC) [PDF]. Retrieved from https://drive.google.com/file/d/12DxgoStq6cu58SIMcZTp9K9daPDYjX 82/view, https://archive.is/6Rh48.

2017, January

Brigitte Fortin retired (co-author of the "Go-Live" Recommendation, February 18, 2016).

The percentage of employees with errors in their paycheques reached nearly 60%. According to the Office of the Auditor General, this was a peak[85]. This error rate was causing the backlog of outstanding "pay requests" to grow — payroll staff could not keep up.

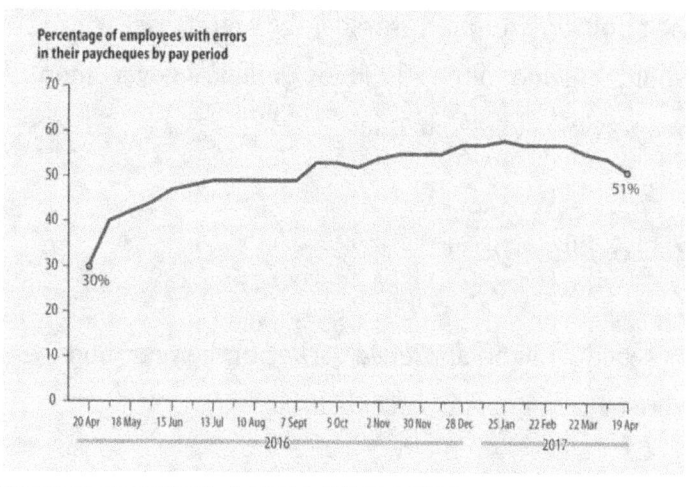

Figure 10: Percentage of employees with errors in their paycheques by pay period. Figure from 2017 Fall Reports of the Auditor General of Canada.

---

[85] Office of the Auditor General of Canada, "Fall 2017 Reports of the Auditor General of Canada to the Parliament of Canada," accessed on March 2, 2023, https://www.oag-bvg.gc.ca/internet/English/parl_oag_201711_01_e_42666.html, https://archive.is/0QRV6.

2017, March

Gavin Liddy was promoted to Privy Council Office.[86]

2017, May

Through an access to information request, CBC (Canadian Broadcasting Corporation) learned that a $13 million contract with Hewlett Packard was under consideration for the implementation of a "Case Management System" to track payroll errors.[87]

(Some argued the work should be done by IBM within the scope of their contract to build Phoenix. It is not clear, to me, how this resolved.)

---

[86] Gavin Liddy. (Accessed April 7, 2023). Gavin Liddy [LinkedIn profile]. LinkedIn. https://www.linkedin.com/in/gavin-liddy-1a7b7650/, https://archive.is/AuM3P.

[87] CBC News, "Public Service Investigation into Phoenix Leak Widens to Other Departments," CBC News, May 3, 2017, https://www.cbc.ca/news/politics/public-service-investigation-into-phoenix-leak-1.4086197, https://archive.is/Zp3LD.

2017, June

The backlog of pay issues grew to 500,000. The number of public servants affected exceeded 150,000.[88]

Canada's Auditor General reported that 51,000 federal employees were *underpaid* by a combined $228 million — so far. And 59,000 employees were *overpaid* by a combined $295 million. They forecast that it would take more than five years to process all currently pending transactions (not including new/subsequent errors that would inevitably follow).

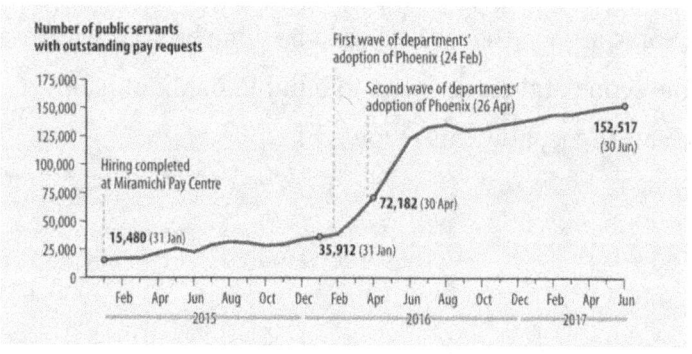

Figure 11: Number of public servants with outstanding pay requests. Figure from 2017 Fall Reports of the Auditor General of Canada.

---

[88] Office of the Auditor General of Canada, "Fall 2017 Reports of the Auditor General of Canada to the Parliament of Canada," accessed on March 2, 2023, https://www.oag-bvg.gc.ca/internet/English/parl_oag_201711_01_e_42666.html, https://archive.is/oQRV6.

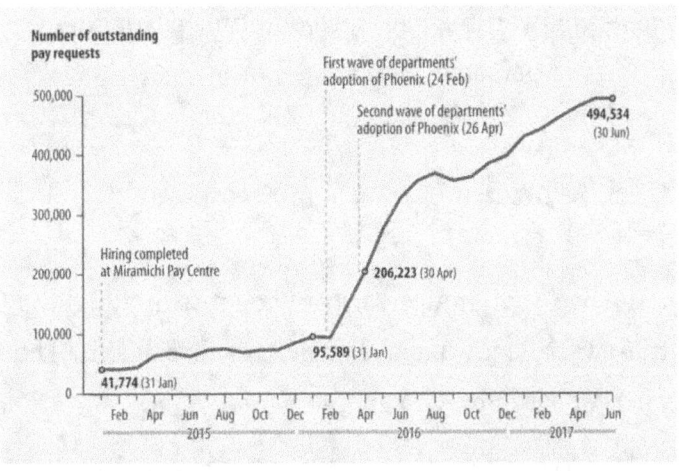

Figure 12: Number of outstanding pay requests. Figure from 2017 Fall Reports of the Auditor General of Canada.

2017, August

Judy Foote retired (Public Services and Procurement Minister, the unit in charge of Phoenix).

And 300 payroll staff were re-hired. (Remember, they were laid off during the effort to centralize the operation in Miramichi.) It is argued at least 200 more were needed and the Treasury Board approved $142 million to cover the cost.

To entice former compensation advisors, and appease current payroll staff, Canada's government offered an increase in overtime pay and a one-time payout of $4,000 per person.[89]

2018, February

On the two-year anniversary of Phoenix's first flight, Ottawa Citizen journalist James Bagnall, called it "The Two-Year Tire Fire".[90]

The backlog of outstanding pay errors reached 633,000.

The Auditor General estimated the costs could exceed $1 billion. *(Little did they know.)*

And as we might have expected, people started calling for Phoenix to be replaced. The Ottawa Citizen editorial board was among the early adopters of this idea[91] with an article called *Start From Scratch on Phoenix*.

---

[89] CBC News, "Ottawa Offers Perks to Attract Phoenix Staff," CBC News, August 24, 2017, https://www.cbc.ca/news/politics/ottawa-offers-perks-to-attract-phoenix-staff-1.4266509, https://archive.is/DiEP8.

[90] Bagnall, James. "Risks unheeded, journey without end: The seeds of the tortured Phoenix pay project were planted three decades ago." Ottawa Citizen, 24 February 2018, https://ottawacitizen.com/news/politics/risks-unheeded-journey-without-end-the-seeds-of-the-tortured-phoenix-pay-project-were-planted-three-decades-ago, https://archive.is/vK758.

[91] "Editorial: Start from scratch on Phoenix," Ottawa Citizen, January 24, 2019, https://ottawacitizen.com/opinion/editorials/editorial-start-from-scratch-on-phoenix, https://archive.is/x1tiC.

(Spoiler alert: I do not subscribe to this foolish idea. See upcoming chapters called *Possible Futures* and *Next Gen HR & Pay System*.)

2018, March

Budget 2018 committed $452.9 million in new funding.[92]

- $16 million "to work with experts" on "a way forward for a new pay system".
- $431.4 million over six years for additional staff.
- $5.5 million to increase capacity at Canada Revenue Agency.

2018, April

Quebec's Superior Court authorized a class-action lawsuit[93] against the federal government. Allegedly:

---

[92] Canada, Government of. "Budget 2018." Government of Canada, February 27, 2018. https://www.budget.canada.ca/2018/docs/plan/budget-2018-en.pdf, https://archive.is/DrYqA.

[93] Sarailis. Phoenix pay system problems. https://sarailis.ca/en/phoenix/, https://archive.is/UVkov. Accessed March 4, 2023.

"...the Government of Canada failed to fulfil its obligations towards its employees during the implementation of the Phoenix pay system and in its management of the problems that ensued. The action seeks compensation for the employees affected by the implementation of the Phoenix pay system starting on February 2016."

2018, July

The Standing Senate Committee on National Finance released a detailed report called: *The Phoenix Pay Problem: Working Toward a Solution.*[94] To save you having to read it, I shall share highlights:

They revealed that the Public Service Pay Centre included 1,455 compensation advisors. *(If you are keeping track, that was more than ever!)*

They calculated $953.9 million had been spent so far — including the funds approved in the government's 2018 budget. They estimated "the government will incur approximately $2.2 billion in unplanned expenditures"

[94] Standing Senate Committee on National Finance. "Phoenix Pay Problems: Working Toward a Solution." Senate of Canada, 2018, https://sencanada.ca/content/sen/committee/421/NFFN/reports/NFFN_Phoenix_Report_32_WEB_e.pdf, https://archive.is/sA7Wy.

to "operate and stabilize" Phoenix. (That was over and above the $309 million "planned" budget.)

They were complimentary toward the payroll employees in Miramichi. They were critical of the managers and executives.

And, though I will address this point in more depth in the upcoming chapter called *Possible Futures*, the senators also recommended replacing Phoenix. The idea was gaining momentum and, in fact, the government announced funding in the 2018 budget to plan for the "next generation of the federal government's pay system".

2019, March

Budget 2019 committed $554.2 million in new funding.[95]

- · $21.7 million to "address urgent pay administration pressures".
- · $523.3 million (over five years) to provide "adequate resources".

---

95 Canada, Government of. "Budget 2019." Government of Canada, March 19, 2019. https://www.budget.gc.ca/2019/docs/plan/budget-2019-en.pdf, https://archive.is/ZzDR4.

- $9.2 million to the Canada Revenue Agency to "quickly and accurately process income tax reassessments" for federal employees.

2020, March

Christopher Nardi of the National Post reported "after weeks of intense pushback from employees and unions" the government abandoned a plan to onboard 3,500 RCMP civilian members to Phoenix.[96]

2020, July

Strangely, Ottawa Citizen's James Bagnall declared "Phoenix Pay is finally working". The headline was intriguing, but wrong.

Bagnall's article was prematurely optimistic — he tried to weave a story of "long-delayed hope" using PSPC's data showing that the backlog of outstanding payroll

---

[96] Christopher Nardi, National Post, "RCMP civilian members hit by Phoenix pay system problems," National Post, accessed on April 08 2023, https://nationalpost.com/news/rcmp-civilian-members-phoenix-pay-system, https://archive.is/cQeMg.

errors had shrunk to its lowest point since Phoenix's birth in 2016.[97]

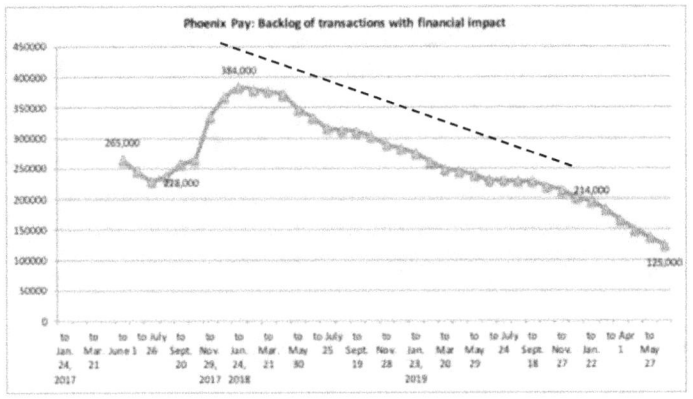

Figure 13: Table included by James Bagnall, data credited to Public Services and Procurement Canada.

Bagnall had good reason to be optimistic. The data clearly show a trend in the right direction.

But the lull was short-lived. Let us revisit that chart including 2023 data. (See next chart.)

[97] James Bagnall, "Believe it or not, Phoenix pay is working. Now what?," Ottawa Citizen, July 28, 2020, https://ottawacitizen.com/business/local-business/believe-it-or-not-phoenix-pay-is-working-now-what, https://archive.is/Lrqpt.

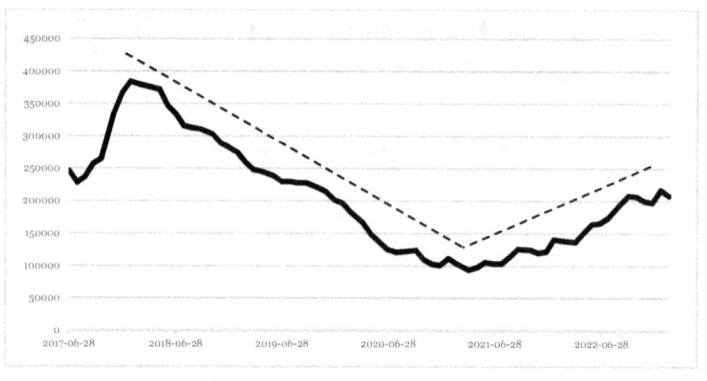

Figure 14: Same dataset as in Figure 13, provided by 'Open Government' initiative, through 2020.[98]

[98] Government of Canada, Treasury Board of Canada Secretariat, "Federal public service employees paid through the Phoenix pay system, 2016 to 2021," July 20, 2021, https://open.canada.ca/data/en/dataset/794d237b-3299-43e1-85ab-98fdc0c6dad9.

The Trudeau Era, 2nd Term

In October 2019, after four years of a Liberal majority government, it was time for Canadians to head back to the polls. Trudeau's support was in decline and the Tories won the popular vote. Lucky for Trudeau, his party held on and returned to office as a minority government.

***

Luke Bryan was *Knockin' Boots* while Lee Brice spread a *Rumor*. Ariana Grande had a *Boyfriend* and Billie Eilish had a *Bad Guy*.

And at the 7th Canadian Screen Awards in Toronto, *Gord Downie's Secret Path in Concert* won two awards. But he was not there to receive them — the legendary Gordon Downie had died in 2017.

Also, in this upcoming term, Eddie Van Halen would play his last concert.

May they rest in peace.

***

Trudeau's 2nd term was brief and the world was spinning, it seemed, out of control. For better or worse, the ongoing Phoenix tragedy rarely reached the news cycle.

2021, April

Budget 2021 committed $92 million in new funding.[99]

- $46 million more (over two years) to "eliminate the backlog".
- $46 million more (over two years) to "stabilize" and employ additional compensation advisors.

---

[99] Government of Canada. "Budget 2021." Department of Finance Canada, April 19, 2021, https://www.budget.canada.ca/2021/pdf/budget-2021-en.pdf, https://archive.is/tzhwa.

The Trudeau Era, 3rd Term

Note quite two years into his 2nd term, Justin Trudeau thought voters would reward him with a majority government amidst the throes of a global pandemic. He called an election and hoped to gain 13 (or more) seats. Instead, he lost more of the popular vote but, miraculously, gained five seats. It was not enough to form a majority.

The results were nearly unchanged from the 2019 election. Canadians found themselves with the same minority government but a new $600 million bill to pay for Trudeau's snap election.

***

Dua Lipa was *Levitating* and Ed Sheeran shared with us his *Bad Habits*. Keith Urban had *One Too Many* while Chris Stapleton was *Starting Over*.

2021, September

Blacklock's Reporter shared news that, as a form of compensation for hardship, $2,500 was paid to approximately 175,000 Canada Revenue Agency employees "whether they were underpaid in the first place".[100]

The total cost of this payout is estimated to be $437.5 million.

2021, November

Hundreds of millions were committed by Canada's Treasury Board for damage claims. The funds were not allocated voluntarily, but in response to litigation by the public sector union and other parties. The Secretariat explained:[101]

---

[100] Blacklock's Reporter, "CRA Compensated Everyone," accessed March 4, 2023, https://www.blacklocks.ca/cra-compensated-everyone/, https://archive.is/yid28.

[101] "Government of Canada Launches Severe Impacts Claims Process under Phoenix Damages Agreement with Public Service Alliance of Canada," Newswire.ca, January 30, 2020, https://www.newswire.ca/news-releases/government-of-canada-launches-severe-impacts-claims-process-under-phoenix-damages-agreement-with-public-service-alliance-of-canada-859286647.html, https://archive.is/CoNiq.

"This claims process reflects elements of the Phoenix damages agreement[102] signed with PSAC in October 2020, and complements existing claims processes for out-of-pocket expenses and financial costs, which continue to be available to public servants including those represented by other bargaining agents.

The Treasury Board of Canada Secretariat is also working in collaboration with PSAC to launch a claims process in December 2021 for former employees to receive general damages compensation for stress, aggravation, pain, and suffering..."

These amounts were in addition to damages paid to federal public servants in 2019 and 2020. Nobody can be faulted for losing track, so let us take stock of all

---

[102] Treasury Board of Canada Secretariat. (2020, February 21). Phoenix pay system damages agreement. Government of Canada. https://www.canada.ca/en/treasury-board-secretariat/topics/pay/phoenix-pay-system/phoenix-pay-system-damages-agreement-2020.html, https://archive.is/IPyuB.

(known) damages paid so far (credit to Bill Curry and Kristy Kirkup for their helpful estimates):[103]

- $160 million was paid in 2019 as compensation for damages.
- $400 million was paid in 2020 as compensation for damages.
- $165 million to be paid in 2021 as compensation for damages.

2022, February

Important to note that legal recourse for affected employees is *not* limited to litigation with their employer. For example, Blacklock's Reporter posted news of a federal employee who lost their home in a legal battle with her bank.

> "A federal employee who fell in default on home loans due to the Phoenix Pay System fiasco has lost a court case with her banker...[she] was so

---

[103] The Globe and Mail. "Ottawa paid out $400-million in Phoenix pay compensation to federal employees, documents show." The Globe and Mail, 20 Dec. 2021, https://www.theglobeandmail.com/politics/article-ottawa-paid-out-400-million-in-phoenix-pay-compensation-to-federal/, https://archive.is/hf0C2.

distressed she quit her job to cash out pension funds to pay the debts she owed."[104]

2022, April

Budget 2022 did not mention Phoenix.

2022, October

Errors continued with federal employees' paycheques and more than $400 million in overpayments had yet to be collected. The Auditor General of Canada warned parliamentarians they "might be running out of time to collect on overpayments".[105]

2023, February

In a press release, PSAC (the union representing federal employees) accused Canada's government of

[104] Blacklocks.ca. "Phoenix Victim Loses House." October 19, 2021. https://www.blacklocks.ca/phoenix-victim-loses-house/, https://archive.is/HCsDD.

[105] Global News. (2022, October 27). "Phoenix system overpaid bureaucrats by $500M — now it's time to claw that back: watchdog". Retrieved March 3, 2023, from https://globalnews.ca/news/9231644/phoenix-pay-system-auditor-general/, https://archive.is/5ykwW.

being "heavy-handed" in their effort to collect overpayments.

> "The Pay Centre is racing against the clock to recover these overpayments because there is a six-year limitation period for overpayment recoveries, after which they have no legal right to recover the funds."[106]

2023, March

Budget 2023 committed $1.038 billion in new funding.[107]

- $517 million for 2023.
- $521 million for 2024.

---

[106] Public Service Alliance of Canada. (February 20, 2023). Phoenix overpayments: More letters expected this year and how PSAC is taking action. Public Service Alliance of Canada. Retrieved March 18, 2023, from https://psacunion.ca/Phoenix-overpayments-more-letters-expected-this-year-and-how-PSAC-is-taking-action, https://archive.is/GB07J.

[107] Department of Finance Canada. (2023). Budget 2023. Retrieved from https://www.budget.canada.ca/2023/pdf/budget-2023-en.pdf, https://archive.is/9FpTH.

How Much Has It Cost?

I assert that the knowable costs exceed $4.2 billion already (see next page). But I estimate the total burden on taxpayers will reach tens-of-billions and the total cost of the Phoenix catastrophe is unknowable.

First, because it is difficult to draw a boundary around the expenditures specifically related to Phoenix. Second, because only some expenses are reported publicly. For example, legal settlements are not always disclosed; budgets are often shuffled and renamed, and direct payments to contractors may be redacted to protect "Cabinet Confidences".

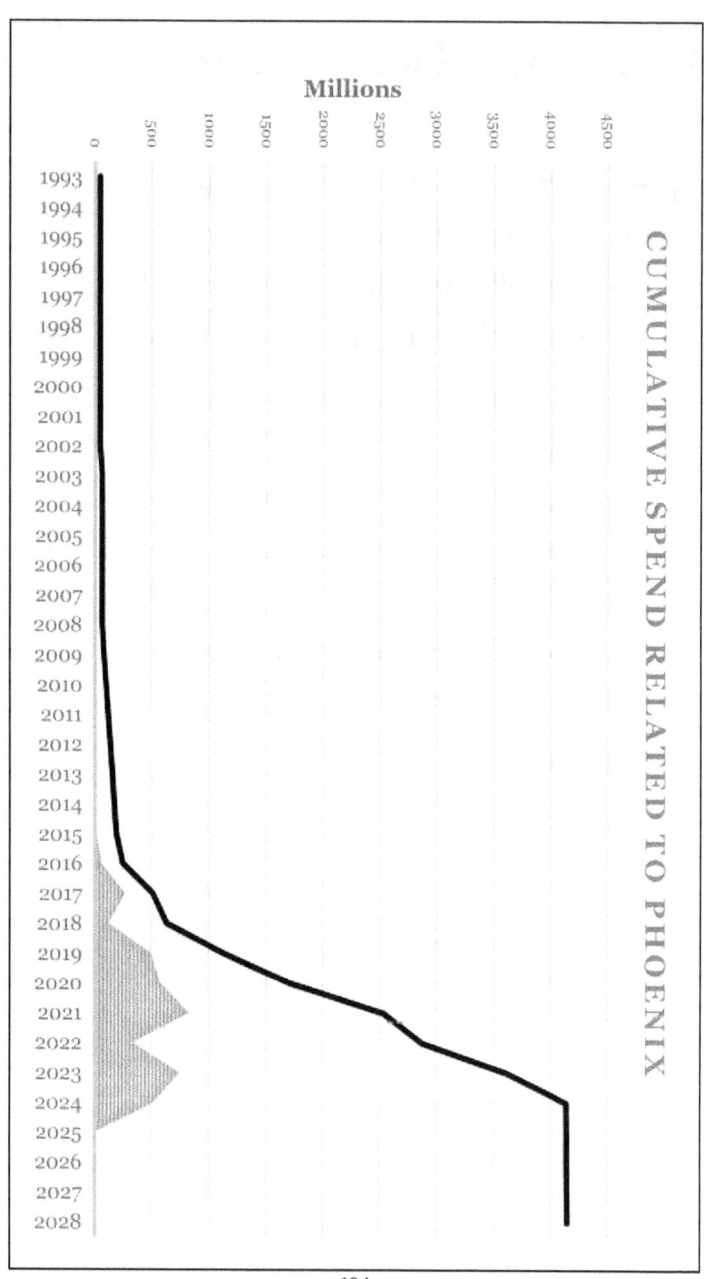

CUMULATIVE SPEND RELATED TO PHOENIX

Millions

Figure 15: Data table showing costs per annum.[108]

Data table (years as rows; costs per annum). Blank cells indicate no reported cost.

Year	Accenture Contract	Accenture Settlement	Centralize Pay Centre	Phoenix/PeopleSoft	CBSA Implementation	CRA Implementation	CSC Implementation	INAC Implementation	Parks Canada Impl.	RCMP Member Pay Impl.	RCMP for PSEs	Overpayments	Case Mgmt System	Budget Shuffle	More CRA Staff	"NextGen" Procurement	"Adequate Resources"	Damages Settlements	NextGen	Damages Settlements2	$2500 * CRA	Ceridian NextGen	NextGen Pension Interface	PSDPT	"for SSC…next-gen pay"	"Maintain Resources"	Year Sum	Cumulative Sum
1993	45																										45.0	45.0
1994																											45.0	45.0
1995																											45.0	45.0
1996																											45.0	45.0
1997																											45.0	45.0
1998																											45.0	45.0
1999																											45.0	45.0
2000																											45.0	45.0
2001																											45.0	45.0
2002		20																									20.0	65.0
2003																											0.0	65.0
2004																											0.0	65.0
2005																											0.0	65.0
2006																											0.0	65.0
2007																											0.0	65.0
2008			17.6																								17.6	82.6
2009			17.6																								17.6	100.1
2010			17.6																								17.6	117.7
2011			17.6																								17.6	135.3
2012			17.6																								17.6	152.9
2013			17.6																								17.6	170.4
2014			17.6																								17.6	188.0
2015				23.3	5.4	13.1	1.1	8.6	1.9	2.1	1.3																56.7	244.7
2016												88	13	142													268.3	511.0
2017															8 / 2.8 / 71.9 / 16												122.0	633.0
2018																9.2 / 21.7 / 104.7 / 160 / 117.1			400.5								495.3	1128.3
2019																				165 / 437.5							577.1	1705.4
2020																											827.2	2532.5
2021																					23 / 23 / 23 / 23	2.1	3 / 44 / 60	2.4 / 4.5			338.6	2871.1
2022																						2.1			52 / 517		747.7	3618.8
2023																						2.1				521 / 523.1	523.1	4141.9
2024																						2.1					2.1	4144.0
2025																						2.1					2.1	4146.2
2026																						2.1					2.1	4148.3
2027																						2.1					2.1	4150.4
2028																						2.1					2.1	4152.5

Additional column headers present in the source table: "Explore new system", "More Payroll Staff", "More CRA Staff2", "More Pay Admin", "Damages Settlements3", "Eliminate the Backlog", "Stabilize", "RCMP HR/Pay E2E", "Enhance Claims Process", "TC Systems Revitalization".

Notes:

[108] David Sabine. (2023). Phoenix Costs [Microsoft Excel spreadsheet]. Retrieved from https://scrumworks834-my.sharepoint.com/:x:/g/personal/david_sabine_scrum_works/EcygCL3JX3JHtjrNaNDT6zwBOSlkXV0AXcDLC_xphe_oqQ?rtime=OXhz0RY520g, https://archive.is/957QJ.

- In the chart above, I spread some of the budgets "over *x* years" if the government indicated as such. Please refer to the link in the footnote for the source spreadsheet.
- I included the Accenture contract (and settlement) — they are the ashes from which Phoenix rose.
- The SI Systems and Gartner reports are not included. (I could not find evidence whether the costs of those reports were included in the original Phoenix allotments.) I would estimate their costs at less than $1 million.
- Overpayments totalling $88 million were reported in 2017. It is not clear whether those amounts were included in subsequent announcements. (e.g., Perhaps in the $142 million budget shuffle described in the Senate Report?)
- It cannot be known the sum of overpayments collected in future — and some overpayments will never be collected due to a six-year statutory limit.
- $13 million for a Case Management System was allegedly under consideration (for Hewlett-Packard) in 2017. It is not clear how those funds

were categorized and reported. (I did not include
this amount.)

· An official budget was not released by Canada's
government in 2020. Expenditures in that period
were gathered from other sources.

Opportunity Costs

I will leave it to you to imagine the countless things
Canada's government could have done with $4.2
billion. I will say only that the opportunities were
infinite — and the reality is such a disappointment.

Hidden Costs

It is not inexpensive to mobilize Canada's Senate to
inquire, examine, and produce a formal report. It is not
without cost to dedicate to this topic thousands of
person-hours in Parliamentary committees. And we
will never know how much was spent to maintain old
systems well beyond their intended expiry date. And we
will never know the cost of countless legal battles past,
present, and future.

The Human Toll

Consider so many individuals affected, each circumstance so unique and bizarre. I can only imagine the plight of each federal employee; what it must feel like.

Cruel, I suppose.

I am reminded of reading Franz Kafka as a younger man — surreal and nightmarish situations featuring characters trapped in bureaucratic systems. Kafka's tone is always so matter-of-fact and detached, eerily in contrast to the absurdity and hopelessness of the plot. As in *The Trial*, in which an innocent man is arrested and subjected to an incomprehensible legal process; Canada's Phoenix project makes Kafka's fiction seem tame and unimaginative.

Also consider the combined effect of hundreds-of-thousands of federal employees underperforming due to stress...for years seemingly without end. Even as I write this page, the backlog of payroll errors is in the hundreds-of-thousands. And that backlog is replenished every two weeks as new paycheques are issued.

Who Is To Blame?

There is a long list of people whose salaries the Canadian taxpayer should no longer support.

Whether they are guilty of world-class incompetence or they knowingly pushed the unfinished system into use, there is plenty of blame to go around.

It is important we approach blame with care and empathy. When I say "blame" I do not mean to provoke witch hunts and lynchings. Rather, there is utility in learning which actions and decisions caused damage. It is reasonable to expect people to take responsibility for their mistakes — and if they lack self-awareness or courage to do so, then blame can be a tool for promoting responsibility, accountability, and improvement.

I would rather avoid blame — I take no pleasure in it. But our subject is the Phoenix payroll tragedy; it is among the most visible and devastating failures of Canada's government. "Who to blame" is a question many have asked. I would fail in my duty as an historian if I were to neglect the topic.

Is Justin Trudeau's Government To Blame?

Somewhat. But not really.

I count myself among the millions of Canadians who are *beyond* tired of Trudeau's scandalous party. But they are no more at fault than anyone else.

True that Trudeau himself, and many in his cabinet, held the requisite authority to stop the rollout of Phoenix if even a single bureaucrat or consultant had advised it. But there is no evidence of such advice.

And hypothetically, even if someone had informed Trudeau of the true condition of the project, what incentive would he have had to push the brakes? If the rollout went smoothly, his government could declare a "quick win" early in their first parliamentary session. And if the rollout did *not* go smoothly, he could blame it on Stephen Harper. And, politically, it is better to be seen *managing a crisis* than to be caught *mismanaging a project*.

I believe the parliamentarians of early 2016 simply trusted (too much) the advice given to them by bureaucrats.

Is Stephen Harper's Government To Blame?

Sorry to disappoint, but no.

Like Trudeau before him, Harper can be blamed for little more than trusting the managers responsible for the project. All evidence suggests that Harper approved the budget and otherwise stayed out of the way.

When bureaucrats told him their plan, or when they changed their plan, he accepted it as such. Like when they told him their planned launch date in 2015 was unrealistic and needed to be delayed to 2016, it appears he did not argue. In fact, he visited Miramichi, explained the delay, and reset expectations. (This was not without political consequences — and I give credit where it is due.)

Nonetheless, it became fashionable for Trudeau's MPs and journalists to point fingers and make baseless claims implicating Harper's government. For example, Liberal MP Scott Brison in May 2017:[109]

---

[109] House of Commons Canada. (n.d.). Government Operations and Estimates Committee Evidence - OGGO (42-1) - No. 88 - House of Commons of Canada. Retrieved March 16, 2023, from https://www.ourcommons.ca/DocumentViewer/en/42-1/OGGO/meeting-88/evidence, https://archive.is/kWk1M.

"...it is [Harper's] government that is responsible for laying off 700 compensation professionals who processed the pay in the public system. It was a bad decision, which left our government short of human resources..."

The implication was that Stephen Harper had set in motion a series of events that, like the Earth's rotation and the rising of the sun, was unstoppable by the Liberal MPs — they were powerless victims of bad inheritance.

James Bagnall of the Ottawa Citizen wrote:

"With the human resources already trimmed and allocated, there was no going back.

There was no Plan B."[110]

Well, of course there was a plan B!

Not only was it possible to "go back" and re-hire hundreds of payroll staff, but that is precisely what happened starting in summer 2016.

---

[110] Bagnall, J. (2018, February 24). Risks unheeded, journey without end: The seeds of the tortured Phoenix pay project were planted three decades ago. Ottawa Citizen. Retrieved March 2, 2023, from https://ottawacitizen.com/news/politics/risks-unheeded-journey-without-end-the-seeds-of-the-tortured-phoenix-pay-project-were-planted-three-decades-ago, https://archive.is/vK758.

It is upsetting that 700 payroll staff were laid off or otherwise shuffled into other roles — but any serious person who appreciates facts knows that the decision to downsize and centralize was not Harper's. Those recommendations were key features of the business case presented in 2009. And more than a third of the 700 staff terminated during the cutover to Phoenix were fired by Trudeau's government long after Harper left office. MP Alupa Clarke clarified:

> "...the process of firing 700 people was perhaps started by [Harper's Conservatives], but the 250 people who were fired between February and April are part of those 700... [Trudeau's Liberals] should have stopped that, just like Harper did after the election when he said that we would postpone the firing of those 250 people and postpone the launching of the system because it wasn't ready...
>
> [The Liberal] government decided, at the same time as it launched the Phoenix system, to fire those 250 people...That's the reality, and Canadians need to understand that."

In the whole mess, I argue there was one *potentially* controversial policy decision on Harper's desk: the new location of the centralized payroll office. That decision would concern the Prime Minister's office no matter who was PM at the time. Miramichi was a likely candidate and uncontroversial — any Prime Minister might have made the same decision. The only reason anyone *pretended* that Miramichi was controversial was the fact Harper had previously committed to ending the long-gun registry (a program popular among Harper's political rivals).

Are the contractors to blame?

More than a little, yes.

Some contractors are more, *je ne sais quoi, noteworthy* than others. For example, ADGA mostly stayed under the radar but IBM was in the hotseat for a few years.

ADGA

Not much is written in the public record about their involvement — they did not make it into the headlines. If the evidence had raised more questions, I may have investigated more. (Please forgive me, it may be a weakness of this book.) I suspect they acted like a recruiting agency to provide staff *ad-hoc*: coordinators, requirements gatherers, testers, *et cetera*.

SI Systems

This group of project management consultants did precisely what they were hired to do. And they did it competently. If they are to blame for anything, it is they should have rejected the work altogether on account of the fact it was utterly pointless. Their work achieved nothing of value for the Canadian taxpayer.

I did not find evidence revealing their fee, but if they were paid $1, it was too much. They were the commercial equivalent of a magic mirror:

> Oh, great mirror on the wall
> tell us our bonus will be tall!
> Never mind reality, report our story,
> our loyalty to the plan is our glory!

Gartner

I wish the language of Gartner's report was stronger.

They had the evidence, knowledge, and opportunity to shout from the rooftops. Their report could have been more abrupt, jarring, alarming. Instead, the nature of the crisis was obfuscated by their palatable tone. But it is difficult to find fault in their work and cast blame in their direction. They were hired to review the system; they did so; they reported their findings.

Can we fault the consultants for being too polite? Too deferential? Was their report so "professional" and reserved that it obscured the truth?

Only in *hindsight* did journalists and parliamentarians perceive Gartner's report as a damning criticism. But in early 2016, the report served to calm the nerves by showing a (supposedly) pragmatic path through the imminent launch. Paraphrased, their report amounts to: "Go for it. Take one step at a time. And hold on tight, it will be a bumpy ride."

Oracle

Oracle is paid jaw-dropping amounts by Canada's federal *and* provincial governments. The result? They can afford to employ an army of sales representatives and lobbyists to peddle their hard-to-use, hard-to-customize, expensive-to-maintain software system: *PeopleSoft*.

PeopleSoft is the name of a software product. The first version was released in 1989 (by a company of the same name) after more than two years of development. The product is/was advertised as an "all in one" system for the management of HR, payroll, finance, sales, *et cetera* (all the core business administration functions).

In the early years of the company, they worked aggressively to establish a foothold in the enterprise market. Their strategy was so successful that the much larger Oracle Corporation bought the company in a hostile takeover in 2005.

There is nothing magical about the technology — every computer science graduate could build it (given enough time). Its basic design is what is known as "client-server" architecture: all the data and most of the code (the business logic) is housed in centralized databases and "servers"; then, "client" applications are run on each computer used by administrative staff.

PeopleSoft is positioned as a "commercial off-the-shelf" "turnkey" product — it purports to be complete and fully-functional "out of the box". But it is also positioned as "customizable".

And there is the conundrum. By any standard, it is difficult and expensive to extend and customize. In fact, much of the technology is proprietary and Canada's government not only pays for the use of *PeopleSoft* but must pay for a suite of related tools just for the privilege of customizing it for their needs: *PeopleTools*, for example, is a proprietary suite of components; and *PeopleCode* is a proprietary scripting language.

Each time the core *PeopleSoft* product is updated by Oracle, many customizations are rendered obsolete or inoperable. Canada's government therefore finds itself in a continuous cycle of updating and rebuilding their custom extensions. (So much for a "turnkey commercial off-the-shelf system that works out of-the-box".)

Oracle Canada, predictably, considers the federal government a target customer. Their lobbyists and sales personnel are aggressive and would have been influential in the years leading up to 2009 when the business case was submitted *and* again when the subsequent RFPs were published.

Can we fault Oracle for successfully selling their product to gullible bureaucrats?

Some would argue they exaggerate the capabilities of their software and set unrealistic expectations about its customizability and total cost of ownership. Others would say the fault lies squarely with the federal employees who are bewitched by those sales ploys.

Whether you conclude Oracle is to share in the blame, one this is certain: the game is rigged by both parties (the software vendor and the bureaucrats) to extract as much money as possible as fast as possible from Canadian taxpayers. It can make a person sick just thinking about it.

IBM

IBM is to be blamed, plenty, but not the lion's share.

IBM was contracted to provide the database and application servers, configure and manage the *PeopleSoft* installation(s), and provide development teams who were tasked with writing, deploying, and testing the many customizations.

IBM's reputation and brand are strong and choosing their services is seen as a safe and reliable decision. "Nobody gets fired for hiring IBM", it is often said. As such, we might say they used their privileged access to influence the procurement process and win the Phoenix contract. We might say they exaggerated their skill and capability. We might say they made commitments to a timeline without knowing it was impossible.

And those things *were* said. In a news story from September 2017, Julie Ireton wrote about IBM's 1,700 page contract obtained by CBC News. Here are highlights from her article[111]:

The contract was worth $185 million. Talks began at $5.7 million but the costs grew as 39 amendments were made to the scope of the project. As scope increased, so too did IBM's price.

Interesting, but not surprising, the government reserved the right to extend the contract for up to 20 years. Roman Klimowicz, former analyst with the Treasury, identified a potential conflict of interest whereby IBM had significant control over defining the project, then implementing it, then fixing it. He told Ireton, "the statement of requirement could leave loopholes, could leave escape avenues in it...IBM basically has an open bag of money to help themselves to."

IBM defended themselves with a response to her article saying, "IBM was hired to install and customize third-party commercial payroll software the Crown had selected. IBM delivered its scope of work per the Crown's specifications." And their claim was supported

---

[111] Julie Ireton, "Phoenix pay system: IBM signs contract with Ottawa to join public servants in fixing mess," CBC News, September 28, 2017, https://www.cbc.ca/news/canada/ottawa/phoenix-ibm-contract-union-pay-government-1.4295827, https://archive.is/iUHyO.

by related statements from Allan Cutler, a procurement expert (it is said he is the person who blew the whistle in 1990s about the Liberal sponsorship scandal), he told Ireton the contract "clearly states the government is responsible for critical decisions... mismanagement of these critical items is strictly the responsibility of the government."

Perhaps we can fault IBM for their part in communications breakdown, setting unrealistic expectations, and producing defects. But their job (here's one way to think of it) was *not* to implement a pay system; rather, to follow the government's instructions how to implement a pay system. The distinction is important. Perhaps they didn't do the job well or within the time frame they promised, but they did the job asked of them.

IBM even tried to petition the bureaucrats to delay the launch. (We will soon see evidence of this in an upcoming section.)

But Julie Ireton also pointed out a curious anomaly: IBM was the only company to bid on the government's RFP.

When millions of dollars are up for grabs for a government contract, would you agree that is highly unusual?

Perhaps the explanation for this is found in documents from ten years earlier: do you recall from a previous chapter that IBM was hired to produce a report in 2007 called *Pay Benchmarking Study*? Ireton referenced that document in her 2017 article — that study influenced the design of the government's Business Case and the RFP process.

That is a polite way of saying the truth — let me try something more direct: the authors of the Phoenix Business Case let IBM's cocks into the henhouse — and the cocks did what cocks will do.

Please know I am not casting a derogatory slur upon IBM or any of their personnel. I am merely using an apt analogy to highlight the fact *Canada's federal bureaucrats opened the gate!* Did they think the wolves had become sheep? Did they think the sharks had become vegetarians?

Cock a doodle do, as they say.

To close the book on IBM, I will conclude:

- The money paid to them is regrettable. I stand with every taxpayer fuming mad that IBM happily drank pure gold from the firehoses meant to put out Phoenix's flames. I wish they would return every dollar.
- IBM has nurtured cosey relationships with high-ranking government officials — taxpayers who have questions about ethics violations and conflicts of interest are wholly justified.
- But to conclude IBM is to blame requires the far-fetched belief that some other vendor, or the government's own internal IT staff could have conducted the project successfully.

***

One thing for sure, and I must make clear, any blame cast toward IBM is to be directed at their sales staff, account executives, and managers. The strata of software developers are surely *not* to blame. They are mere cogs in a larger machine. (Please don't accuse me of dehumanizing them, I merely point out the nature of their work environment.)

Developers in an environment like theirs, act on instructions laid out before them. Buried under mountains of virtual documents are their marching orders: screen needs a button that says "Submit"; form needs a field for a telephone number; user must be able to change their password, *et cetera*. The Phoenix pay system is the sum of all those instructions.

Yes, each individual developer may be guilty of low motivation, bad communication, maybe they even produced a bug here or there, but their responsibility and authority is limited by IBM's organizational design and the contract they served.

We must look now to the people who authorized and controlled the IBM contract.

Are the bureaucrats to blame?

Absolutely yes.

I am not alone with this opinion. But, before I am criticized for writing an entire book only to reach the same conclusion spouted by a thousand others, I will introduce an issue that has escaped everyone *so far:*

from my vantage point, the question is not whether the bureaucrats are to blame. The question is *when*.

Let us briefly revisit the point of no return in 2016 and the approval of business case in 2009.

2016

There is widespread agreement that terrible mistakes were made by senior bureaucrats in January through April of 2016. You and I have already dedicated a few pages to that period in a previous section.

There exists a list of senior managers involved in the project who had the opportunity to do the right thing for the Canadian taxpayer and the federal employees who would bear the greatest burdens. I would include in that list the most senior bureaucrats of PSPC and PWGSC (those who governed the project) but I would also include those who managed each and every department affected by the Phoenix rollout. (I am referring to those who undertook the "Readiness Assessment" in late 2015; who found the system *not ready*; then failed to courageously defend the personnel in their department.)

To all of them I would say: What benefit to the citizens of Canada is your salary and the office you hold if you are unwilling or otherwise incapable of exercising its authority when it matters most? Of 37 million Canadians, *you* were among the few dozen with the information and authority to have prevented Phoenix from catching fire.

Even Canada's senate concluded that the fault lay with departmental managers:

> "The causes of the failure are multiple, including, failing to manage the pay system in an integrated fashion with human resources processes, not conducting a pilot project, removing essential processing functions to stay on budget, laying off experienced compensation advisors, and implementing a pay system that wasn't ready."[112]

Again, for anyone who pays little attention to politics, that paragraph is as damning as it gets in Westminster officialdom. And they didn't stop there, the senators all but named names. For example, they told of behind-

---

[112] Standing Senate Committee on National Finance. The Phoenix Pay Problem: Working Toward a Solution [PDF file]. Senate of Canada, 2018.
https://sencanada.ca/content/sen/committee/421/NFFN/reports/NFFN_Phoenix_Report_32_WEB_e.pdf, https://archive.is/sA7Wy.

the-scenes conversations between executives at IBM and the officials in PWGSC:

> "Regan Watts [of] IBM Canada, said that IBM representatives had tried to warn the government as late as January or February 2016 that neither the software nor the pay transformation process was ready."

And my favourite quote of the senators' report was a statement by the Auditor General:

> "Phoenix was an incomprehensible failure of project management and oversight, which led to the decision to deploy a system that was not ready."

***

A lot has been said of the obvious failures of managers in 2016. But most critics focus on the infinite ways the Phoenix project could have been *better managed*. "If only they had delayed the launch", they say. "If only they did more testing", they conclude.

I think that level of analysis is short-sighted and I want to spill some ink to explain why the Phoenix project should never have happened in the first place. By early

2016, the Phoenix system was simultaneously *unusable* and *too big to fail* — delaying its launch would have caused a cascade of failures across other systems that were interdependent on Phoenix and/or its personnel. How exactly did Canada's government find itself in such a predicament? To answer that question, let us return to 2009.

2009

I believe most journalists and parliamentarians who followed the story believe Phoenix ignited in February 2016 — as though a bomb was suddenly detonated. But, as you and I have studied, the root cause is much deeper and much older.

The business case submitted in 2009 was called the *Initiative to Fix the Pay System*. There were two crucial errors in judgement made by senior bureaucrats at the time:

- · First, the notion that "fixing" the pay system meant that the existing technology had to be *replaced*.

- Second, the notion that the existing technology could be replaced in a single blow by a "commercial off-the-shelf" (COTS) product.

Those two assumptions were forged over the course of many years leading up to 2009 and were grounded in nothing more then a prevailing mentality based on faith, myth, wishful thinking, superstition, hubris, perhaps hope.

Those assumptions led Canada's government to approve the business case and pour money, time, and personnel into the project.

Phoenix ignited in 2009, and like a long-running fuse, the inferno quietly grew for six years as the project became so massive and so interdependent that some of the most accomplished experts in the field would grow afraid of stopping it.

Possible Pasts

There are many possible pasts, but one is particularly interesting to me. This is the past where Canada's government replaced their *legacy project management* methods, before their tech.

This is the past where IT managers in the 1980's made a goal, not to *replace* their systems, but to create a supportive engineering culture and *evolve* those systems with the changing times.

This is the past where bureaucrats proposed a decade-long Waterfall project to install a "commercial off-the-shelf system" and were told to take a long walk in the snow. Rather than "one and done" replacement of entire systems, IT managers prioritized flexibility and adaptability, continuous improvement, and refactoring.

In this past, the payroll systems were (deliberately, not haphazardly) a *potpourri* of software tools: no single point of failure, some off-the-shelf, some tailor made, some home grown, some old, some new.

The IT managers were granted sufficient resources to maintain the tools and they fostered engineering practices that achieved high quality code (e.g., test-driven development, collective code ownership, continuous integration). They negotiated a high-level architectural vision and guardrails to ensure cohesive design and interoperability.

IT consultants were employed strategically, not to augment internal staff at crunch time before a deadline as is often done now, but to invoke fresh ideas and spur innovation. Their perspective as outsiders was valuable, they stirred the pot just a little, and prevented internal staff from thinking too narrowly and becoming too insular.

Compensation advisors knew the tools well because they, all along, were involved in their continual renewal. New feature requests would lead to incremental adjustment: an upgrade here, some automation there. The payroll personnel knew the IT personnel by name. By involving the end-users in the design and development, the system was tailored to the specific needs of the organization. It was *fit for purpose* and updated through small, reversible, low-risk steps.

***

How could this possibly have worked? You may ask.

Then I: *how could it not?*

And, frankly, all the evidence is on my side.

First, the alternatives have proven expensive at best, catastrophic at worst.

Second, it is important to remember the low failure rate of the pre-Phoenix software systems. In fact, those federal departments who opted out of the Phoenix launch have maintained their RPS (Regional Pay Systems) throughout. Those systems are ancestors of the pre-Phoenix era — and last I checked they've *not* been in the news! They have quietly delivered millions of paycheques without much *ado*.

Even as the Phoenix business case was negotiated in 2009, bureaucrats and parliamentarians disparaged their "40-year-old" systems, forgetting (or misrepresenting) the fact that those tools were functioning quite well. We saw testimony at committees in 2007 that efforts to "strengthen and modernize" those systems were ongoing. We heard testimony that compensation advisors knew the systems very well. We heard that the *real* trouble, according to payroll staff, was the complexity of collective agreements and the meddling of managers who refused to hear solutions proposed by their employees.

The pre-Phoenix IT solutions continued to operate at a high success rate with a consistent number of personnel until 2016 when Phoenix was released.

True, we saw testimony that the "old" systems had grown difficult to maintain. Difficult. Not impossible. And I argue that is because they were *chronically underfunded*. I am not suggesting the Canadian taxpayer was underfunding the IT operations, generally — I only suggest that the moment a manager or executive set their sights on "the next big project" they shut down all other proposals.

To every improvement idea: "No, that will get replaced when project X goes live." To every feature request: "No, that requirement will be in project X." The prospect that "a big solution is on the horizon" causes managers to ignore inexpensive, incremental advances.

In the 80's, managers turned their attention to "pay systems modernization" leading to the contract with Accenture. In 2007, managers turned their attention to the Phoenix business case. In 2018, to the "Next Gen" replacement. Meanwhile, the "old" systems continued to work quietly in the background.

Since the 1960's, deep in the bowels of Canada's federal IT and payroll departments, and in the remaining few departments who still depend on their RPS, are unsung heroes who reliably deliver paycheques to the right people for the right amount at the right time. On a shoestring budget and *sans* fanfare, they dedicate their care and attention while managers overlook them. The unsexy work of gradually improving their aging payroll system does not render headlines nor promotions. It is thankless at best and often entirely invisible to the management strata.

So, in the *actual* past, developers have been fixing, integrating, automating, solving problems, and building tools. But in our *imaginary* possible past, they were doing so with full support.

Next Gen HR & Pay System

It is not the purpose of this book to analyze the new project. I will dedicate only a few pages to share context and key events.

***

By early 2018, nearly two years since Phoenix was released, people started to talk about "replacing" the system. Already, a half-billion dollars had gone up in flames, the system was throwing more errors than ever before, lawsuits were underway, and key personnel were taking early retirement or being shuffled into new jobs.

It was total chaos.

We cannot fault anyone for letting their imagination wander — "replacing Phoenix" was surely a tempting prospect, but it was also important (politically and practically) to give the option some consideration.

However, we should always be careful not to make rash decisions in the midst of crisis. Or as they say: don't go grocery shopping on an empty stomach.

The Ragnarök Myth

(Please, my dear reader, I did not set out to write a book of mythology. But in my research about the Phoenix, I was led to these amazing stories that are not only *fun* but applicable.)

Norse mythology tells of a most catastrophic event in which the world will be destroyed and reborn in a cycle known as Ragnarök. It is foretold there will be a great battle between the gods and the giants, in which many of the gods will die. *(Now, get this...)* The world will be consumed by *fire* and *water*, and from the ashes of the old world, a new generation of gods will emerge.

I, of course, do not believe Ragnarök is upon us! But *wow!* Our story almost writes itself:

- Fire? (The Phoenix?!)
- Water? (The Waterfall?!)
- New Generation of Gods? (Next Gen HR & Pay?!)

Through the ages, people tell stories about their fears and hardships — evidently, the human experience in the 21st century is not so different than it was in the 8th century.

***

Some parliamentarians and bureaucrats (those closest to the Phoenix) must have felt their world was consumed with bad news, blame, fear. It would be accurate to say they were in "a great battle".

Perhaps to cope, we will discover they were easily captured by the idea that Phoenix was of an *old* ilk and their urgent imperative was to raise a new generation.

The result: Canadian taxpayers must finance two distinct streams of activity. The raging fires of Phoenix needed (and still need) to be tamed; and an entirely new project was launched called *Next Generation HR & Pay*.

Agile Procurement

Something changed over the winter holidays leading into January 2018. Suddenly everyone in Ottawa was talking about "agile procurement".

It certainly was a busy time in the "agile community" (if there is such a thing) and for *me*, personally, as a purveyor and teacher of "Agile" ideas and practices.

In early 2018, I was founder and Executive Director of the Ontario Scrum Community® and we were preparing Canada's first-ever Regional Scrum Gathering® in Toronto.[113] I was regularly teaching six to eight Scrum training courses each month through 2017 with 20 to 30 people in each class. I taught classes in Ottawa, Toronto, Montreal, Vancouver, and a few private classes for select government departments. Interest within Canada's largest employers had grown to peak levels.

The "Agile Manifesto" was nearing 16 years old and I believe the ideas (e.g., iterative & incremental development, cross-functional teams, customer & user centricity) had crossed the chasm of the technology

---

[113] https://davidsabine.ca/scrumgathering

adoption lifecycle and were well on their way to reaching late majority.

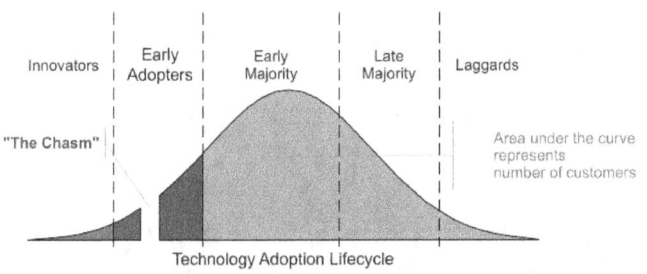

Figure 16: Theoretical Technology Adoption Lifecycle.[114]

Early adopters (I consider myself in this category) of Scrum, XP, DevOps, Cloud, *et cetera*, learned from the innovators; then early adopters recruited others; by 2010 we were seeing evidence of early majority adoption; and given enough momentum, it was inevitable the ideas would reach into the halls of government.

When the buzzword "agile" started showing up in government committees, we must conclude the idea had reached even the late adopters and laggards. And to be honest, and perhaps I cannot hush the cynic in me, I am undecided whether this is a *good* thing for

---

[114] Chelius, C. (2009). Technology-Adoption-Lifecycle [Diagram]. Wikimedia Commons. https://commons.wikimedia.org/wiki/File:Technology-Adoption-Lifecycle.png.

Canada's government. I want to be cautiously optimistic. But the devil is in the details and we will have to wait a few years to learn whether anything more than the buzzwords will stick.

One of those buzzwords is "agile procurement".

To understand "agile procurement", let us first consider the Agile myth. And as we know, all myths begin with a question. In the case of Agile, the question was something like, "given that we are uncovering better ways to develop software, how can we help others to do it?"

The answer is *in* the question — the question implies a competition: what does it mean to uncover "better" ways? Better than *what?*

Well, better than the prevailing practice of the era, namely: the Waterfall. But not only the Waterfall. There was/is a competition between two large sets of ideas.

In one set are lightweight practices like Scrum, XP, Kanban, DSDM, Lean Startup, Feature-Driven Development, Impact Mapping (and many more); in the other set are intensely bureaucratic patterns like "Big-Design-Up-Front", sequential engineering, phased/gated governance, Rational Unified Process, and SAFe.

The Agile Manifesto is simply a reflection of those contrasting sets of ideas — as in the focal point of the document, four value statements, as follows:

> **"Individuals and interactions** over processes and tools
>
> **Working software** over comprehensive documentation
>
> **Customer collaboration** over contract negotiation
>
> **Responding to change** over following a plan
>
> That is, while there is value in the items on the right, we value the items on the left more."[115]

So, to expand Agile mythology to involve "procurement", we might simply imagine an opposite to the prevailing, intensely bureaucratic approach. Let us try together:

The prevailing procurement strategy in Canada's government presumes the end state of the project can be predicted in advance; it demands a pre-determined

---

[115] https://agilemanifesto.org/

sequence of gated activities; it expects comprehensive documentation and tightly controlled processes; it limits customer collaboration; and changes late in development are abhorred and often penalized.

What if?

What if we accept that the end state of the initiative is unknowable? Therefore, we must devise a way of writing contracts that enables us to respond to change and ensures collaboration between the people creating the software and the people using the software. And the success of the initiative is measured not by documents, based entirely on conjecture and cover-your-ass officialdom, but by the frequent/incremental delivery of high-quality well-functioning software?

That — if you can imagine it — would be "agile procurement".

***

So, what were parliamentarians talking about in early 2018? Let us have a look...

2018, February

The OGGO committee invited industry experts to discuss challenges that small and medium enterprises face in the government's procurement process. Among them was Dan Murphy to discuss "an agile approach to procurement".[116] Dan made an appearance at committee in October 2017 as parliamentarians were showing some interest in the topic.

In February, Dan returned among other witnesses. The committee heard ideas to make the government's RFP process more lightweight, and how doing so would help engage smaller, more nimble companies. They heard of ways to de-risk large projects by breaking them into smaller investments. They heard of ways to make the procurement process more collaborative.

Andy Akrouche, witness, provided historical context to remind that "agile procurement" is not a silver bullet. He posed an interesting question:

---

[116] House of Commons. (2018, February 13). Standing Committee on Government Operations and Estimates evidence - OGGO (42-1) - No. 119 - House of Commons of Canada. Ourcommons.ca. https://www.ourcommons.ca/DocumentViewer/en/42-1/OGGO/meeting-119/evidence#Int-9972907, https://archive.is/QUmxS.

"...which part of this agile procurement have we not tried before?

...for those of us who are old enough, the BDP process, the benefit-driven procurement process...this was back in 1994. It was an outcome-based process, exactly the same stuff we're talking about here...

Next we came up with something called CPP, which is a common-purpose procurement, which is exactly the same stuff. In the style of Dragons' Den or Shark Tank...

Of course, we have the JSP, which is joint solution procurement, which really comes down to a very competitive process between the final two vendors...

We have performance-based contracting, which came into the federal government from Australia and which we actually do right now. Most of the contracts that are coming out of DND are all performance-based contracts...

We have smart procurement...designed to really increase this collaboration throughout the whole competitive process...

Now we have commissioning, which is really another form of performance-based contracting, the old ASD model in a combination with the JSP. Now we call it commissioning...

If all we want to talk about is having agile procurement, which is really a combination of all these different things that we've done in the past, my view is that they haven't really worked very well. The outcome we've been looking for has been very elusive, because I think we're not addressing the real problem...The real problem lies in the relationship management."

***

It is clear in the evidence that parliamentarians and bureaucrats were growing entranced with another version of the Phoenix myth — they imagined an entirely new, off the shelf, centralized system could replace the existing software. (Sound familiar?)

This time, however, their faith in the Waterfall was shaken — the Waterfall myth provided an answer to the question, "how will we manage this project?" For the "Next Gen" system, they looked to new mythology to answer that same question. They found an answer in "agile procurement" — they imagined a great battle (the Ragnarök) between rival companies that gives way for a new generation payroll system. They would hire multiple vendors to showcase their existing tools, in competition.

2018, November

Budget 2018 committed $16 million in funding "to work with experts" on "a way forward for a new pay system". In an OGGO committee meeting, parliamentarians would learn how those funds were being used. MP Scott Brison explained:

> "[we are] leading the development, at Treasury Board, of the next-generation pay system. We're using an agile, digital procurement approach that is actually going to see working prototypes being tested by public servants in the coming months..."[117]

---

[117] Standing Committee on Government Operations and Estimates, 42nd Parliament, 1st Session, November 1, 2018, https://www.ourcommons.ca/DocumentViewer/en/42-1/OGGO/meeting-25/evidence#Int-9030239, https://archive.is/tFcRx.

2019, June

Canadians learned more about the procurement strategy for the "next generation" system[118] as three companies were selected to replace the Phoenix.

Julie Ireton of CBC summarized the strategy:

> "While only one of the companies will eventually be given the task of designing and implementing the new system, the other two firms might still be brought in to provide certain components, depending on the evolving needs of the hundreds of federal departments.
>
> The next stage will be developing a pilot project...until the old system can be phased out."

The three companies selected where SAP, Ceridian, and Workday.

And another clear difference in procurement strategy was highlighted. Ireton explained, "Unlike during the development of Phoenix, the government's own IT staff have a role to play this time, according to Debi Daviau,

---

[118] CBC News. (2019, June 12). Companies square off in competition to replace Phoenix pay system. CBC News. https://www.cbc.ca/news/canada/ottawa/companies-competition-replacement-phoenix-pay-system-1.5172249, https://archive.is/Fo9nx.

president of the Professional Institute of the Public Service of Canada (PIPSC)."

2020, March

Canada's Government announced $117 million was committed to the effort.

And SAP was selected as the front-runner to build Phoenix's replacement.[119]

President of SAP Canada, Andy Canham, said: "Team SAP looks forward to continuing to work with public servants, unions and employees on a modern, digital solution...one that will meet the needs of the Federal Public Service and its employees."[120]

***

[119] Treasury Board of Canada Secretariat. (2020, March 6). Moving forward with NextGen. [Blog post]. Retrieved from https://tbs-blog.canada.ca/en/moving-forward-nextgen, https://archive.is/ndK6b.
[120] "SAP selected by government to test complexities of payroll and HR requirements." IT World Canada. Accessed April 4, 2023, from https://www.itworldcanada.com/article/sap-selected-by-government-to-test-complexities-of-payroll-and-hr-requirements/428234, https://archive.is/vm0H5.

If you are taking notes, as I did, to discover what "agile procurement" means to Canada's Government, we have seen evidence that they (1) introduced competition in the bidding process; (2) they requested "pilot" projects and demonstrations from multiple vendors; (3) and despite having selected a primary vendor [SAP] the other two companies in the great battle [Ceridian and Workday] would remain on the list of qualified suppliers for any future HR and payroll work with the government.

It remains to be seen if this strategy is ultimately successful. Perhaps let us reserve judgement.

2021, September

Canadians would learn that the great battle was not yet over! SAP was announced just months prior as the first victor (see previous page). Had they been dethroned by their rival, Ceridian?

What I am about to tell you is that Ceridian won the contract to replace Phoenix — but truly, I do not know whether SAP was ousted or is still involved. It is difficult to know — news of the Next Gen HR & Pay initiative is scant since March 2020. For example:

- The Treasury Board of Canada Secretariat used to keep a blog where project updates were published. The most recent post was three years ago: March 6, 2020.[121]
- An internal wiki called GCCollab that used to publish frequent updates has been virtually static since mid-2020.[122]
- And budget reports do not provide sufficient detail.

And, my dear reader, I do not want to give the impression that something nefarious happened — so, I will merely tell you the facts and you can draw your own conclusion. The following facts were reported by Sean Silcoff and Chris Hannay of The Globe And Mail:[123]

---

[121] Treasury Board of Canada Secretariat. (2021, March 6). NextGen HR and Pay. TBS Blog. https://tbs-blog.canada.ca/en/nextgen-hr-and-pay, https://archive.is/eXpR4.

[122] GCCollab. (n.d.). NextGenHRandPay-ProGenRHetPaye. GCCollab Wiki. https://wiki.gccollab.ca/NextGenHRandPay-ProGenRHetPaye, https://archive.is/ToTeU.

[123] The Globe and Mail. (2021, September 21). Federal government selects made-in-Canada software to start replacing Phoenix pay system. Retrieved April 11, 2023, from https://www.theglobeandmail.com/business/article-federal-government-selects-made-in-canada-software-to-start-replacing/, https://archive.is/hPauk.

- One month after the announcement awarding SAP the victor, Ceridian hired Gianluca Cairo. He was formerly the Chief of Staff to MP Navdeep Bains.
- Federal Ethics Commissioner Mario Dion reportedly cleared Cairo, finding no conflict of interest.
- Navdeep Bains had, just previously, announced his retirement from political life — he announced he would not run in the 2021 election.
- By summer of 2021, Canada's Government awarded a contract to Ceridian to start replacing Phoenix. But news of this contract was hidden from Canadians during the 2021 election campaign. David Ossip, CEO of Ceridian, said in an interview the news was subject to "blackout periods with regard to the election...", and he said Justin Trudeau's government "didn't want it to be viewed as anything to be influenced by the election".
- The implementation by Ceridian was scheduled to start with the Canadian Heritage department. The Minister of Canadian Heritage was MP Steven Guilbeault until September 2021. Then

MP Pablo Rodriguez took over the portfolio in October.

- Public reporting of the project ceased (the internal wiki has no activity, and the Treasury's blog went dark) — it appears control of the project changed hands.
- Ossip reportedly spoke of the contract as "a multidecade partnership and collaborative effort..." and "obviously we expect to be very successful".
- Ceridian has since opened a state-of-the-art office on the waterfront in Singapore.[124]
- A spokesperson for Shared Services Canada (a department under PSPC, the same department responsible for procuring Ceridian) reportedly assured "the contract decision was made by the department, not Liberal cabinet ministers."

***

[124] https://twitter.com/dossip/status/1513071235520819200

That is all I can report of the NextGen HR & Pay initiative. Few details are known of the project since mid-2021. Perhaps "no news is good news"?

Possible Futures

No More One-And-Done Projects
No More Large Scale "Replacements"

The worst possible future is where Canada's government continues the *status quo*.

The Phoenix mess is not unique. Hundreds of Phoenix-sized projects continue to happen, many with dire consequences including cost overruns and *questionable* value. The Waterfall and Phoenix mythologies are strong — Canada's government is addicted to large projects aimed at replacing existing systems.

Advice:

> "Why do 'fix all the problems at once' projects have such a track record of ten and hundred million dollar craters?
>
> Compounding risk.
>
> The more problems you try to solve at once, the more things can (and will) go wrong. Chances are that eventually the risks are going to catch up with

you. You can only dodge snake eyes so long."

— Kent Beck[125]

Another Phoenix-sized mess is inevitable. Only a matter of time. The *status quo* has a lot of inertia as illustrated in the Senate Report of 2018 where they provide this opinion:[126]

> "...the government should explain to Parliament the options it is considering to replace Phoenix, the costs of these options, and how it intends to avoid repeating the mistakes of the Phoenix pay system...
>
> ...we are dismayed that this project proceeded with minimal independent oversight..."

That advice guarantees another catastrophe. They never questioned the supposed need to "replace" the system and they suggest the solution is *more* bureaucracy. "Independent oversight", they say. That always means more bureaucrats who don't have skin in the game — that is *not* the answer.

---

[125] Mechanical Orchard. (2023, April 20). Features and Design: Why Not Both. Mechanical Orchard. https://www.mechanical-orchard.com/post/features-and-design-why-not-both, https://archive.is/QOnws.

[126] Standing Senate Committee on National Finance. The Phoenix Pay Problem: Working Toward a Solution [PDF file]. Senate of Canada, 2018. https://sencanada.ca/content/sen/committee/421/NFFN/reports/NFFN_Phoenix_Report_32_WEB_e.pdf, https://archive.is/sA7Wy.

But I have an idea! Avoid repeating the mistakes of the Phoenix pay system by avoiding giant replacement projects.

And notice, Phoenix did not *replace* the old systems — many of the RPS remain to this day! And the "Next Gen" product does not *replace* Phoenix. Canada's government finds itself in the very situation it wanted to avoid — it is simultaneously maintaining multiple, half-baked systems.

Here are a few unavoidable truths Canada's government must learn (the following points are summarized from John Gall's *The Systems Bible*[127]):

·   New systems generate new problems.
·   The old system is now the new problem.
·   The ghost of the old system continues to haunt the new.
·   A complex system designed from scratch never works and cannot be made to work.
·   A complex system that works is invariably found to have evolved from a simple system that worked.

---

[127] Gall, J. (2002). The Systems Bible. 3rd edition of Systemantics. Refer to Appenix 1. General Systemantics Press.

Simplify All Collective Bargaining Agreements

This is a contentious issue and if it were easily resolved, it would be by now. Right?

Collective bargaining is inescapable so long as there are collective bargaining units. And it is clear in the testimony by compensation advisors that collective bargaining agreements grow in number and trend toward complexity.

Canada's government maintains an impossible labyrinth for compensation advisors and software developers alike. The error rate will be high unless one of two outcomes are achieved:

- Either the collective agreements are simplified;
- Or the software and its users achieve sufficient quality that all 80,000+ regulations are perfectly navigable for every employee for every paycheque. (After $4.2 billion, that outcome remains elusive. How much more will it take to prove it's a fool's errand?)

It must be there are incentives in the system of government employment that increase the number of contracts and their regulations over time. To set a new course toward less complexity, those same incentives would have to be studied and carefully modified. That is a subject to fill many volumes — it is beyond the scope of this little book.

Change CapEx/OpEx Fiscal Habits

A volunteer group called Ottawa Civic Tech[128] keeps a repository of the Government of Canada's large IT projects.[129] The dataset includes only the projects that departments have self-reported since 2016:

- 1,126 projects are larger than $1 million.
- 324 projects are larger than $10 million.
- 42 are larger than $100 million.
- 3 are larger than $0.5 billion.

Canada's government spends, per year on IT projects, roughly the Gross Domestic Product of Jamaica.[130]

---

[128] https://ottawacivictech.ca/, https://archive.is/yXGzg.
[129] https://large-government-of-canada-it-projects.github.io/, https://archive.is/rhbZc.
[130] International Monetary Fund. (2022). World Economic Outlook Database, April 2022. Retrieved from https://www.imf.org/en/Publications/WEO/weo-database/2022/April/weo-report, https://archive.is/ObDdv.

I don't know precisely how the Treasury Board of Canada categorizes those large projects as CapEx[131] or OpEx[132], but let's take a guess. Which of these do you think they prefer?

- "We have a new $500 million asset on the balance sheet."
- "We spent $500 million on IT operations."

***

I'll use a few pages to explain CapEx and OpEx and will weave the topic (hopefully) toward yet another explanation why Canada's government is obsessed with buying "replacements" for systems they already own. If you are familiar with CapEx and OpEx concepts, feel free to fast forward to the next section (***).

And here we go...

Operational expenses look like *costs* on a company's balance sheet. They are simple tax deductions like office expenses, utilities, or rent. Employee salaries, for example, are considered operational expenses (unless

---

[131] Capital Expenditure.
[132] Operational Expenditure.

there is good reason to claim otherwise, read on). And in the production of software, the greatest costs are salaries.

But capital purchases function differently.

Imagine a company worth $0 earns enough to buy an asset worth $1 million. That company's value has increased to $1 million. (Actually, that's debatable, but let's keep this simple.)

The company's $1 million capital can be used as collateral against new debt. So, imagine the company arranges for a loan and the interest they pay on that loan is tax deductible. And they can use that loan to invest in a new asset, or to pay salaries. In other words, the company can use its capital to take new risks such as borrow money to expand the company and hire more people.

Furthermore, their $1 million asset depreciates over time. The depreciation of that asset is also tax deductible over the course of several years. That's good news.

But the bad news is the asset loses value. Eventually, the value of that asset will fall to near $0. With some luck and/or strategic asset management, the $0 asset may still be useful to the company. Maybe the asset was a computer that still functions well or a car that still runs reliably. (Notice the usefulness and value of the asset are two different things.)

Consider the incentives: human effort is the biggest cost in the development and maintenance of software tools, and salaries are usually considered operational expense, and OpEx offers none of the tax strategies of CapEx. Meanwhile, purchasing a software system is CapEx. The system increases the apparent value of the company, it can be used as collateral, its depreciation is tax deductible.

Are you thinking what every CFO already knows? These incentives can cause companies to *buy* software systems rather than develop in-house.

Now, before I am criticized for over-simplifying, companies don't *always* simply buy an asset (such as a software product), sometimes they produce it themselves, in-house, then creatively account for the expense so they can employ those same tax and debt strategies.

The language in tax codes has expanded to enable this and a common phrase used to describe this accounting technique is "new capability". The logic goes like this: a capital expenditure (like a new computer or tool) becomes valuable (an asset) to the company because it enables a new capability within the company — the new asset has the potential to improve the company's operations, enhance its products or services, or create new revenue streams.

That rationale offers the possibility of declaring *some* of the cost of IT development as CapEx. And the simplest of strategies is, behold, the Waterfall. As follows:

(OpEx)
Plan ↘

    (CapEx.............................)
    Code → Test → Deploy ↘

        (OpEx..................)
        Operate/Maintain

The strategy is as common as it is unimaginative. It is useful, though often problematic. At worst, this fiscal habit impedes the quality of software when managers impose the pattern in large batch, big project delivery. Often, to make financial reporting easy, they divide the work across departments and assign large batches of work. Like this:

- The architects and designers will work for 6 months. (OpEx.)
- Then coders and testers will work for 6 months. (CapEx.)
- Then the "ops" teams will maintain it forever. (OpEx.)

Division of labour, as above, is optimized for reporting and auditing; it is not optimized for software quality.

But, as we learned during the *Interlude* (see earlier chapter), software quality is improved with iterative and incremental development (IID) patterns. But not all companies learn how to apply their CapEx/OpEx fiscal strategy at a more granular level that is complementary to IID. I have worked with many teams that practice IID and *some* have had the necessary conversations with auditors, financial controllers, and lawyers to determine the best ways to categorize their activities. The goal is to declare relevant activity as CapEx and the remainder as OpEx.

Here's how it works in a nutshell: the planning, management, and maintenance activities are still

OpEx; and the coding, testing, deploying activities are still CapEx; but the teams deliver features to market in a continuous stream rather than a big batch launch; and they tag the coding, testing, deploying activities on a per-feature basis.

This is not difficult. The harder part is having the right conversations with the right executives (CFO, CTO, Legal) to achieve alignment and training.

(Tip: hire me.)

***

How does all of this apply to Canada's government?

Politically, the optics of Capital versus Operational expenses are asymmetrical. The sitting government (no matter which party holds office) will say they are "*investing* strategically"; while the opposition party (no matter who holds the office) will criticize their opponent for "*spending* recklessly".

Also, Canada's Government is addicted to debt. Deficit spending is fueled by loans from the Bank of Canada — those loans are either backed by bonds sold to investors or backed by assets owned by the government.

Last, Canada's Treasury enforces the Waterfall pattern to make CapEx/OpEx accounting simple. In *A Guide to Project Gating for IT-Enabled Projects*[133], you would notice in the description of "3.7 Gate 6" this subtle information under "Typical input to the review":

> "All sign-offs for user acceptance, production acceptance by operations, security certification and accreditation to go into production, maintenance team acceptance of documentation."

The key phrases are there. Let me translate for those who do not speak *Projectese*: The operations group (paid by OpEx budgets) will accept the asset as is (produced with CapEx budgets); the asset will be deployed and put into production; the maintenance team (paid by OpEx budgets) will accept that they are now responsible for maintaining the asset.

For Canada's government to break its habit of embarking on large IT replacement projects, difficult conversations must occur including treasurers, auditors, and IT project managers.

---

[133] Treasury Board of Canada Secretariat, Information Management: A Common Approach, accessed March 3, 2023, https://www.tbs-sct.canada.ca/itp-pti/pog-spg/irp-gpgitep/irp-gpgitep-eng.pdf, https://archive.is/IM44m.

PODS

Through my research, I repeatedly encountered the concept of "pods".

Pre-2007, groups (pods) of compensation advisors were located across the country and would serve federal employees in their location. By most accounts, that was not perfect but worked well. It worked better than *separating* the staff and we saw evidence that payroll errors occurred more frequently when compensation advisors were organized into silos (e.g., group A shall manage insurance; group B shall manage promotions; group C shall manage overtime, *et cetera).*

The pods concept showed up again in mid-2016 as Phoenix exploded. Cross-functional pods would swarm to put out the flames: a few people from insurance, promotions, salary, and so on, would gather and could tackle a high volume of payroll errors.

MP Carla Qualtrough explained, in March 2018:

> "...we are looking at how work is organized so that transactions can be handled more efficiently. At the pay centre we are piloting a new approach that organizes compensation experts and support staff

into pods that specialize in specific departments or transaction types, and early results are promising.

> ...one of the significant benefits of what we're calling our 'pod approach' is that we are looking at the whole individual in terms of making them whole. We're not just looking at one particular type of transaction for everybody. We're ensuring that when we look at [a person], we address all of [that person]'s transactions."[134]

Aside: this was not a "new approach" as the MP inferred — rather, the pods were a throwback to how compensation advisors used to operate pre-Phoenix.

More about pods was shared in the senators' report:

> "We heard that some progress is being made at the Public Service Pay Centre in part by using 'pods'..."

The senators went further to encourage "managers should listen to employees more in order to maximize the chances of identifying and correcting technical problems". They supported the notion that people

---

[134] House of Commons. (n.d.). Meeting No. 122 - Standing Committee on Government Operations and Estimates. Evidence [Transcript]. Parliament of Canada.
https://www.ourcommons.ca/DocumentViewer/en/42-1/OGGO/meeting-122/evidence#Int-10013916,
https://archive.is/TXwlN.

closest to the work are likely to have valuable ideas to improve the work.

Who knew?!

Consider the word *gemba*: a Japanese term that means 'the real place' or 'the place where the work is done'. It is the place where operators and supervisors work together. It is where opportunities for improvement can be observed firsthand. For example, in manufacturing companies that employ Lean practices, the Gemba Walk is a common management technique: go to where the work happens, observe, ask questions, seek to understand, and listen for improvement ideas.

Foster a Thriving Engineering Culture

The best possible future is one where Canada's government accepts one basic fact: it will issue paycheques forever.

Please hear me out: a core requirement of government is the employment of public servants; therefore, a core function of government is payroll. So long as the government exists it will issue paycheques every two weeks. *Ergo*, make the payroll systems easy to modify and easy to keep up to date.

The question needs to be asked: will the Canadian taxpayer be on the hook for new payroll systems every few years? Must they pay repeatedly for high-risk "replacement" projects? That is the current condition: every time Oracle updates *PeopleSoft*, for example, a cascade occurs of expensive "upgrade" projects. Will the same be true of the Next Gen HR & Pay system?

The government ought to turn a new leaf, the old dog must learn a new trick. I assert their money would be better spent investing in software engineering staff who produce and maintain a purpose-built payroll system, *in-house*. After all, we're not talking about ground-breaking innovative software tools. We're talking about straight-forward computation, storage, and networking.

This only requires a shift in mindset from "fix all the problems at once" projects, to long-term incremental improvement.

Open Letter to Parliamentarians and Bureaucrats

To all Canadians whose T4 income is paid by taxes: You owe it to your fellow citizens to use their money responsibly.

Whether or not you were involved with Phoenix, I hope you will pursue better ways. Please be open about the challenges you face and have the courage to tackle difficult problems. Please earn the respect of all Canadians who provide you their hard-earned money so you may conduct the business of government on their behalf.

To all those in leadership positions guiding large IT projects financed by taxpayers, I hope you have learned lessons from the Phoenix catastrophe. And I hope you are successful in your future endeavors. And when you are not successful, I hope you muster the courage to ask for help or to step aside so others may succeed where you struggle. That is what taxpayers deserve, after all: responsible individuals working in coordination to ensure the government's activities run smoothly and effectively.

And, to the people who crafted the Phoenix business case and project plan, I want you to know that I empathize. I understand. Many Canadians understand. Many are angry and would appreciate seeing a little contrition or perhaps your resignation, but they/we understand. Perhaps you found yourself in over your head? Perhaps you wanted to reign it in as the train began to derail? Perhaps you feel some remorse for the hardships your colleagues suffered as Phoenix exploded? Perhaps you are a victim of your own ambitions? You sought to conduct a giant project with a giant budget and you hoped for impressive results. Well, the results certainly are impressive but not in the way you intended.

Change is required. The *status quo* is, simply, not good enough. I hope this book is valuable and effective. I hope it invokes ideas that will help mitigate risk. I hope it adds to the ongoing discourse so catastrophes like Phoenix can be prevented in future.

Sincerely,
David Sabine

About the Author

David Sabine consults, trains, and leads teams that produce high-quality, large-scale software. He helps managers understand agility at all levels: delivery, leadership, and organizational design.

He works to improve the profession of software delivery whether consulting in the c-suite, embedded with product development managers, or teaching developers new agile engineering practices.

David has worked with startups who produce medical robotic devices, cloud platforms, and AI, as well as enterprises in the areas of retail, energy management, IoT, and finance.

He grew up in the Canadian prairies and has lived and worked in Saskatchewan, Ontario, Arizona, Florida, Bahamas, and Alberta.

David is a management consultant, product & program manager, author, technical coach, and software engineer. He teaches Scrum, Kanban, and is a frequent presenter at conferences. He is Executive Director of Ontario Scrum Community®, a TEDx alumnus, former professional musician, husband, and dad.

David can be reached at <u>davidsabine.ca</u> for media inquiries or consulting invitations.

davidsabine.ca
betterteams.fm
kanban.guide
scrum.works

www.ingramcontent.com/pod-product-compliance
Lightning Source LLC
Chambersburg PA
CBHW070618220526
45466CB00001B/49